Getting Beyond...

Abuse and Codependency

TO ACHIEVE A LASTING RELATIONSHIP

Patsy Buell Stierna

A Memoir

Dedicated to my husband Robert Charles Stierna
for all the love and devotion he gave me for over 50 years.

Door County Natural Creations
Copyright 2022 Patsy Buell Stierna

ISBN 979-8-9862657-0-4

Getting Beyond...

Cover Photo
Dancing to "When I'm 64." Taken at our 25th Wedding Anniversary
June 8, 1992, Described on page 188

"What does it mean to enrich a life? And to survive and heal from personal trials, and then become an inspiration to many? Patsy Stierna has had a remarkable life, and this memoir of her path to a fulfilling life takes the reader on a multi-continent and soul-searching sojourn of discovery, confrontation, and growth that so many of us can relate to and learn from. The story, enriched with simple but important drawings, delves into the intensely personal moments, into life's details, and into the soulful experiences of this remarkable woman. There is love, marriage, and loss, and rediscovery, and in it all is this richness of how Patsy Stierna has become more than she might have imagined. She writes, "I'm no longer an individual soul seeking God, but a human seeking constructive relationships with other humans and the natural world." In her life is uplifting hope and knowledge of the ability for all of us to heal and thrive." - Roger Kuhns

"This is a powerful memoir of a complicated life. It is also a tribute to the resilience of marriage. To say that love endures all things is not enough. This story shows this with clear understandable examples."
- Carrie Sherrill, Door County Poet

Acknowledgements

Thanks to my family and friends for their support and patience with me. A special thanks to my writing groups: the Round Rock Writers' Guild in Austin, Texas, the Write on Writers' group in Door County, and the South Austin Writers' group. Also, The Clearing and my instructors and fellow students in Roger Kuhn's class and the Women's writing class with Judy Bridges. A special mention to the friends and family who gave me a safe place to write in Australia during the pandemic: Walde Breton, Robert Bender and my cousin Cathy Buchanan.

I didn't do this journey alone. It was only with the help of my fellow yoga students, friends, and therapists that I survived and thrived. I wrote this book to honor our journey. To preserve people's privacy, I have changed names or used only first names in most cases. This is a memoir, and it is based on my memories. Some dialogue is made up but retains the essence of how I remember the interactions.

Table of Contents

Introduction

THIS BOOK IS WRITTEN to share my experience, strength, and hope. It is my hope that through sharing, others might learn from my experiences and know that there is a way to achieve true and lasting relationships.

When I was a rebellious teenager, my mother said, "You never listen to me."

I answered, "I do listen, but I have to learn my own way."

It is through sharing our stories that we can learn from each other and get back on our own path through life, learning from our mistakes.

But I wasn't planning on writing this story at all. I was going to write Volume II of *Visions from Two Continents*. After Volume I was published, I went to a writing retreat in Door County. My instructor, Roger Kuhns said, "Make a story arc."

I scribbled one sad incident after another, constantly looking up out the window at the trees waving me on. I was getting nowhere; I made the arc for Volume I. It told the history of the USA and Australia from 1912 to 1955 through the eyes of my mother, Sheila Buchanan Buell. It had a definite story line, goal, conflict, and resolution. Only the resolution in 1955 never happened. Sheila did not take her family back to her home in Australia. Volume II would be a story of depression and disappointment; I couldn't write it.

Roger said, "Tell me about your life."

I said, "Oh, I didn't have a very interesting life. Besides, I got beyond all the problems and I'm happy now."

"Tell me about it. How did you do that? Make a story map of your life," he said, giving me a direct assignment.

I sat down with a large sheet of paper and scribbled an outline of this book, amazed at all the ups and downs, the angels along the way that helped me learn and grow. I shuffled my way into a private meeting with Roger, wanting to hide behind my scribbled story arc. "This is pretty crazy. I don't know if anyone will believe this or want to read it," I said, my eyes averted from his straight-on gaze.

He smoothed the large sheet of paper on the table and read it very carefully. "There is a lot here," he said. His voice resonated with empathy and calmed my pounding heart. "This is the story you need to tell."

The tension in my shoulders relaxed, "Thanks," I said. "I know I need to tell this story. I just wasn't sure when, or if it would be believed."

"Now is the time," he said with a conviction, that hit me with the force to carry it beyond the room, to share it with the class, and with the world.

CHAPTER 1

Beginnings
1947-1963

School Photo, Patsy Age 8

MY OLDER BROTHER, DENNIS, was conceived when my mother was living alone, separated from her abusive first husband. In fact, my father didn't even know he had a son until Dennis was two years old. The first husband pressured her to abort the child, but abortions were illegal, and Mother wanted to keep the baby. When my father found out about Dennis, he helped her get a divorce and asked her to marry him. Of course, I didn't know anything about this until I was grown up; Mother only said, "Dennis and I have a special relationship."

When Mother brought me home from the hospital, it was in the middle of the polio epidemic. Dennis was just four years old. He was stricken with polio, and isolated in the hospital for six months. My mother was not allowed to see him or even speak to him.

Daddy was worried when I was born with a flat nose. He said, "It wouldn't be so bad if she wasn't a girl." Luckily my nose straightened out after a few days. I was "Daddy's Girl" - the only girl between Daddy's two sons. Mother often told me Daddy said, "Oh, how wonderful, a girl, what a help she will be to you." In 1947 most mothers stayed at home, and daughters learned to cook, clean, and sew. I was supposed to help Mother and my brothers.

Eugene, my younger brother, was a surprise, because my parents were in their forties and thought they were too old for another child. He was just too cute, with huge blue eyes, and curly blond hair.

I have idyllic memories of being a little girl on the farm, 640 acres of rich black soil and woods one hour north of St. Paul, Minnesota. Mother was always home, cooking, gardening, painting, or taking me on walks in the woods. When Daddy came home, smiling from working in the fields or in the city fixing apartments his mother owned, he'd spin me around, holding on to one leg and one arm so I could be Peter Pan. I knew my life was perfect. When my college-aged cousins asked what I wanted to be when I grew up, I said, "I never wanna grow up. I want to go to Neverland and live with Peter Pan."

Before Eugene was born, Mother stayed up late at night, making clothes for a surprise. She was gone for a full week in the hospital and came home very sore, and along with baby Eugene, she brought me a "Jenny doll," with a complete wardrobe of tiny new clothes Mother had made for her. She did not want me to feel threatened by this new baby.

I was six when Eugene was born, but when I was seven Daddy became ill with colon cancer. Mother and baby Eugene were at the hospital all the time. Daddy had colon surgery, then the hospital sent him home. Mother sewed me a nurse's uniform so I could help take care of him. I remember wearing it into the bedroom just once. Daddy looked at me, with a sad smile. He could hardly lift his head off the bed. He groaned and cried at night. Mother and a neighbor loaded him into the car and took him back to the hospital.

I never saw him again.

Daddy's death left an unending hole in my heart, and unanswered questions about life and death. I was always looking for a replacement for this lost Daddy. He was an ideal father figure. I never had any teenage conflicts with him, since he died when I was a child.

Mother was in a state of shock and depression, but she had three small children to raise. She sold the farm and purchased a rooming house near the University of Minnesota. She hoped that with the income from renting out rooms and basic social security, she'd make enough money to stay at home with her children.

My brothers, Mother and I lived in an apartment on the first floor. The house had five additional rooms that were rented on the second floor and an apartment on the third floor. Ali, a tall, thin, handsome Egyptian rented the third-floor apartment. He was just a little bit younger than Mother and courted her. Mother perked up from her grief. We all joked and laughed together. Ali was so tall and thin that we called him "giraffe", mother's hair had a streak of white, so she was a "zebra",and little Eugene was "monkey". Ali took us out for root beer floats at A&W. Sometimes I went up to his room and he talked to me as though I was important. He was like a father to me. Mother wanted to marry Ali, but she didn't want to go to Egypt. When I was ten, Ali's visa ran out, and he went back home to Egypt.

Ali left on February 28. On March 3rd a small box stamped LIVE arrived, addressed to "Patsy Buell."

Mother handed it to me, saying, "I think Ali sent this to you from New York."

"To me, really to me?" I unwrapped the outer covering and a note fell out that said: *I tried to send a giraffe, but it wouldn't fit.* We all laughed, remembering his giraffe nickname.

I pulled a little turtle out of the box. I turned him over. "Look, his tummy looks just like the markings on a giraffe's neck. As I held him gently by his shell, he stretched out his tiny arms and legs, pulling his head out of its shell. I kissed his tiny cold head; it was love at first sight.

I named him Turgey and made a home for him in a glass baking dish, with sand, rocks and a bowl to swim in. The pet store carried special turtle food.

The next week, Mother rented Ali's apartment to Heydar who claimed to be a friend of Ali's. When Heydar arrived at our house, she introduced him to me.

"This is Heydar; he is renting Ali's apartment upstairs. This is my daughter Patsy," Mother explained.

My eyes traveled up over a big belly sticking out over Heydar's belt. The corners of his mouth turned upwards in a sly smile as he looked at me. He held out a large puffy hand.

"How do you do?" he asked,—his voice grating against my ears.

I politely put my hand in his, but I wanted to pull it back immediately. Something was wrong, I really didn't like this man, his wide mouth was too big, his teeth too shiny, and his breath reeked of cigarettes. But worst of all was the gleam in his eyes as he looked at me. He was not at all like Ali.

"Come up and visit me," he said.

"Oh, I think that would be nice," Mother answered for me, knowing how much I missed Ali.

After he left, Mother said, "Just be nice, go up and visit him for a while. You could play your flute.

I plodded slowly up the stairs and went into that barren room, gripping my flute like it was a security blanket. I knocked quietly hoping he wouldn't hear me. He opened the door immediately.

"I'm so glad you've come," he said in a soft voice, that made me grip my flute tighter.

I stepped in the room, and he closed the door. I looked on the door for the hieroglyphic wall hanging Ali had there. It was gone. I didn't smell Ali's incense or hear his music. Instead, the rancid smell of cigarette smoke permeated the room.

Heydar's face turned towards me in a sly toothy grin as he said. "I see you've brought your flute, how lovely."

My heart pounded as I politely sat across from him placing my flute on my lap, and my music on the couch. My eyes concentrated on the music; grateful that I didn't have to look at Heydar. I brought the flute to my lips and started to play, *Twinkle, Twinkle, Little Star.* My breath flowed across the tiny hole in the flute, making it sing this simple song.

He listened impatiently then said, "Come sit here," patting his plump lap.

I hesitated, but reluctantly complied. This was Ali's friend; Mother had said to be nice to him. No one had ever said anything to me about good touch and bad touch. As I sat on his lap his hand caressed my private parts. I wiggled to get free.

Heydar held me closer. "Stay still," he ordered in my ear.

The area between my legs felt very warm, and then it throbbed with an intense sensation I'd never felt before. Held there, I stopped struggling. Finally, he let me go.

I grabbed my flute and hurried down the stairs, relieved to be out of there.

The next day he was talking to Mom in the hall at the foot of the stairs that curved up to the rented rooms. Heydar turned to me with that sly smile and said, "Would you come up and play your flute for me?"

I looked down at the floor, I shook my head, quietly saying, "No." Then I glanced at Mother.

Mother's eyes bore into me, "Oh, be polite and go play your flute."

I went to get my flute and my music. I always tried to be good. Ali had always been so nice to us all. I loved Ali. He'd been almost as nice as my father. Now he was gone too, just like my father was gone.

My heart felt heavy as I slowly walked up the stairs to the second floor. Then I turned the corner down the hall to ascend six stairs to a landing. I almost turned around at the right turn of the stairway. Thinking *Mother said go play your flute,* I held my flute close to my chest as I walked up seven more steps to the third floor. I knocked, hoping this time he wouldn't answer.

"Come on in," he said, shattering my hopes.

It felt more like an order than an invitation. The room smelled from heavy male cologne. I held my flute up in front of my chest like a shield, then I sat across from him and started to play it. I'd planned just to play my flute and stay off his lap, but he pulled me onto his lap. I squirmed and tried to get out of his reach. He picked me up and pushed me on the bed, crawling on top of me. As he reached up to unzip his pants, I slid out from under him. I rushed to the door and pulled the handle, but it was locked. I reached up and turned the knob, unlocking it as he struggled to stand up. I leaped down the first steps, turned and ran down more steps to the hall and kept running down the stairs, breathless, into our little apartment on the first floor. Mom saw the look of terror in my face.

"What's the matter?" she asked.

"Heydar pushed me down on the bed and crawled on top of me!"

"He did what?"

"He pushed me down! He tried to take his pants off, but I ran away. I left my flute up there. I don't want to go get it," I said, bursting into tears.

"Don't you worry, Patsy, I'll get your flute back." she said with her teeth clenched. Her eyes flashed.

I followed her out into the hall, but I didn't go up the stairs.

Mother marched up the stairs and banged on his door. "How could you do such a thing to my daughter? You get out of here right now!" I heard her scream at him standing at the top of the stairs outside his door on the third floor.

Mother returned with my flute and said he would never bother me again. I took my flute and held it close to my chest. Now she understood why I didn't want to go up there. I felt safe knowing Mother was going to protect me. Mother didn't talk to me about what had really happened. I heard her talking on the phone.

"That bastard tried to rape Patsy....."

"No, I won't go to the police. You know they'd just blame me. They might even put the children in child protection."

I tried to go to sleep but I stayed awake wondering. *What is rape? It must be very bad if she doesn't even want to tell the police about it.* I didn't ask her about these things either. She didn't want us to worry. She wanted us to be children. I knew we lived from month to month. Basic social security was only $50 per month for each child, plus the income from renting the rooms upstairs. At the end of the month, we ran out of boxed cereal, but she'd grind dried corn into flour and make us delicious waffles, better than any sugary boxed cereal I'd eaten.

The next week Heydar moved out. I never saw him again, but I never forgot what he did.

At the same time, Turgey disappeared. I was frantic. "Mother, we must find him. He'll die without water or food."

We searched everywhere, under the beds, all along the floors. He wasn't found for another week. Eugene found him under the dresser, covered in dust, his little body stiff and cold.

I was faced with the unknowable - death again. My friend Mary went to Catholic school and seemed to know about such things. She and I had been performing funerals for dead birds. I called her and cried into the phone. "My turtle Turgey's died. Could you help me with his funeral?"

"What? A slimy turtle? No way," she said.

I left Turgey's body sitting on the table and went to bed, burying my head into my pillow, my eyes filling with tears.

Mother cleared the table and put Turgey in the garbage. The next morning, Eugene came running into the bedroom.

"Turgey's moving," Eugene said.

"Where? Where is he?" I jumped out of bed and ran into the kitchen.

"He's in the garbage," Eugene said.

I stared at Mother, "Why, why did you put him in the garbage?"

Mother came outside with us to look. Turgey sat on top of a pile of decaying food. His dried-up body had absorbed moisture and was wiggling with maggots.

"Don't touch him." Mother said. "I'm sorry, but he is dead."

When I was twelve my body changed shape. Bumps grew on my chest that got in the way and bounced painfully when I ran. I was just in the seventh grade. My brother Dennis, four years older, always yelled at me. "Go away, you nitwit. You've got no more brains than a nit. You know that's the larva of a flea?" He laughed at me, never saying a nice word. At breakfast he'd stack up cereal boxes, so he didn't have to look at me. I'd try to be tough back, putting boxes in front of my face too, but more than anything I wanted him to like me.

I was very insecure about my changing body I spent every morning staring at my big nose wishing it smaller as I struggled to brush my long frizzy red hair.

Dennis would pound on the door. "Get out of the bathroom."

Mother yelled at me too, "You're stuck-up, spending so much time staring at the mirror."

Late one night when Mother and my little brother were asleep, Dennis opened the flimsy accordion door to my room and whispered, "Shh, don't tell anyone. You're beautiful," softly touching my budding breasts, I couldn't believe my ears.

Me, beautiful? Maybe Dennis did like me. Maybe we could be friends.

Dennis snuck into my bedroom, almost every week, touching me. I never asked him to come to my room; I just lay there still and quiet. I just wanted him to like me. His fingers massaged my breasts and touched my clitoris, a delicious warm feeling spread up into my being, sometimes throbbing as my body shivered in response to his touch. He never tried to crawl on top of me like that awful man, Heydar. He continued to talk nastily to me during the day, but secretly I knew he liked me. This sneaking around was not right, but I thought, *it created a secret friendship, didn't it?*

One night when Dennis was touching me, he said, "Someday, you'll probably need therapy."

I didn't say anything back, and I never spoke to him when he snuck in at night. But I thought, *I'll never need therapy. I'm not crazy.*

Late in my fifteenth year I started to go out on dates, and I woke up to the insanity of my brother sneaking into my room. I told him to stop. I said, "Don't come here anymore."

He just laughed and said, "You like it." And kept right on coming into my room and being nasty during the day.

There was no way that the flimsy accordion door to my room could be locked. One night I whispered, "If you don't stop coming in here, I'll tell."

"You wouldn't dare," Dennis hissed back at me.

So, the next time he did it, I went to Mother. I remembered how supportive she'd been when I was nine and Heydar had tried to rape me. I thought, *she'll help me, I just can't let this continue.*

I nervously walked up to her standing alone in the kitchen, "Dennis keeps coming in my room and touching me. He won't stop," I said quietly.

She turned staring at me. "He what?"

"He comes in my room at night and won't leave me alone!" This time, it burst out of my mouth, and I stood with my hands clenched in fists.

"How long has this been going on?" Mom looked as if fire was coming out of her eyes.

"A... a ...long time," I whispered sadly.

"How could you do this?" She yelled at me. "You knew better when you were nine. How could you allow this to go on?"

"I... I..." I tried to explain, but I couldn't believe my ears. I felt like a porcelain doll that had been broken in two and thrown in the mud. In my mind I'd just wanted my brother to like me. He had disliked me for as long as I could remember.

I bowed my head, totally guilty.

"This will never happen again, do you hear! Never under my roof."

Mother must have spoken to him because it stopped and was never spoken of again. There was always a silent tension between this brother and myself, never a friendship. But I thought the sexual molestation was my fault. I knew I wasn't to tell anyone ever, not even my best friend. Mom said I should have stopped it long ago, so I held the shame for many, many years.

Sixteen

Mother saw sixteen as a pivotal year and took me on a shopping trip. "I want you to have something special this year. We're going downtown and you can pick out one thing, from any store for your birthday." Mother never got me anything new other than shoes. We lived check to check on basic Social Security from my deceased father. No one at school knew Mother found my clothes at the Salvation Army. The clothes she brought home were good brand names, that she cleaned and modified.

We wandered from shop to shop. Dayton's had beautiful windows with mannequins dressed in the latest fashions, then Donaldson's, and finally a small dress shop on Nicollet Avenue. The bell tinkled as Mother, and I were blown in through the door by the bitter March wind. The clerks hovered around us as I pushed through the sweaters on the rack, tired of looking, never finding anything special or inexpensive enough. Although she'd said, "Don't worry about the cost," I did worry. I knew Mother got only $50 a month allowance for me from Social Security. I put on an Angora cardigan sweater with trees woven into the fabric. The price tag said $30, but it was special. She bought it for me. It wasn't just one or two trees but the entire forest of interconnected trunks rising up, brown and green into a blue sky. The peace of the forest covered me and told me my mother really did love me.

A few weeks later I woke up with blood on my sheets. My girlfriends had all started menstruating long ago and talked about it. I'd worried that maybe I wasn't really a girl since they'd all started, and I hadn't. Mother had warned me, "If you wake up one morning with blood on your sheets, don't worry; just come to me. No one told me when my period started, so I thought I was going to die."

It was reassuring to finally be able to join in the complaints about periods with my girlfriends. I was going to be a woman after all.

That morning Mother gave me a pad and a little elastic belt for me to wear under my panties.

Ok, I thought. *This sounds easy, I'll just have to wear those pads once a month.*

But for me, along with menstruation came feelings like I'd never had before. I felt urges surging in my body. I really didn't care about boys before, but now I felt drawn to them in a strange scary way.

I walked to Mother's bedroom door and knocked. When she opened it, I blurted out my confusion in a rush of words, "Mother, I just don't know what to do. I just keep getting these urges, and I don't know how to deal with them."

"What urges?" she asked.

"Well, I'm not sure." I stopped talking and I put my head down. I just stared at my hands. I felt very nervous about asking her about these feelings. She was a woman; she surely must know the answer.

"Sometimes I just feel like throwing myself at a man." I stammered out, not sure still what I was saying, but I knew it was something I shouldn't be feeling by Mom's twisted face. Her eyes glared at me. She said, "Well, you'd just better control it," and closed the door.

I rushed back to my room and collapsed on my bed, first putting my hands between by legs, collapsing into a fetal position, then quickly pulling my hands out to burying my head. My gut hollowed out like it had the day Mom blamed me for Dennis's molestation. *I want to control it but how?*

There's got to be a way to deal with this, I thought. I didn't know what to do with this body. It measured 36, 26, 36 - a perfect imitation of the lusty shape of Marilyn Monroe, the ultimate sex symbol.

To find an answer; I did what any good student would do. I hopped on my bike and rode down University Avenue to the library. It was about two miles to get to the East Hennepin Branch Library. I parked my bike at the foot on the marble stairs and ascended past the huge columns that guarded the entrance. It wasn't the forest that I loved, but those columns gave it an essence of peace, despite the roar of city traffic. Inside, I slowed my footsteps to be sure the librarians didn't give me the shush treatment. I wandered through the stacks of books looking for help. The library had always helped me to get excellent grades; surely it had answers for this.

There weren't many self-help books. I was looking for anything, but not sure what. Emotions swirled inside me. My mind rebelled against these uncontrolled urges bubbling inside me. A large volume appeared before my eyes; I can see it to this day. It was a thick red book with the title VIVEKANANDA: The Yogas and Other Works.

I pulled it down from the shelf. It fell to the floor open to the pages on Raja Yoga. I sat down next to the book, looking for answers. These words jumped out from that page, *Through prana one can control one's body.*

What is prana? I checked it out from the library and fastened it to my bike. When I got home, I carried it quietly to my room. I didn't tell my family or friends about the book. It was my secret weapon, my way to knowledge and self-control. Every evening I read from it, trying to digest the strange words and follow the instructions.

I sat still on the floor, my legs crossed pretzel fashion, and kept my spine perfectly straight as Vivekananda advised. I first covered my right nostril with my thumb and inhaled deeply into my lungs, counting to eight through my left nostril. Then I closed off the left nostril, and let the air flow out from the right, slowly counting to eight, My body relaxed, and those sensual urges dissipated. A smile filled my being, I was in control of my body.

I repeated this exercise five times. Vivekananda said that I should do this four times a day: before dawn, during midday, in the evening and at midnight for 15 days. Despite my best intentions, I always slept through the midnight one, but I did the rest. At Marshall High School the lunchroom clattered around me. "I'm leaving early, going to the restroom." I said to Marie my best friend.

Our table consisted of intellectual outcasts. We spoke of books and classes, not boys and dates, yet I didn't tell them about my new book, it just seemed too weird. I stood up and headed towards the lunchroom monitor, to tell him where I was going. On the way I had to pass a table of senior boys. Jimmy, a boy in my French class, yelled, "There goes Zelda."

My heart pounded, I had no idea why Jimmy called me that, and my eyes avoided the gaze of the senior boys as they giggled at my expense.

In the restroom Darla, one of the popular girls, was staring into the mirror, putting on lipstick, an unlit cigarette dangling from her hand. I snuck past her and squeezed into a stall sinking down on the cold toilet seat. *Om, Om, Om* I repeated in my mind, breathing in one nostril holding my breath, and then letting the air slide slowly out the other nostril. I did it again, and this time my heart rate slowed, my mind calmed. I was ready to face anything.

It became my secret key to knowledge. I wanted to practice everything Vivekananda suggested. I didn't read all 798 pages of tiny print, but I did skim through the entire book, concentrating mainly on the chapter on Raja Yoga. I renewed the book at least 3 times, after which I had to return it before checking it out again a few days later.

Yoga was not a religion, but rather a yoke, a discipline to be practiced. To me it seemed like a yoke of freedom, and maybe it would even lead to my discovering TRUTH, to know the nature of God, and why my father had died. Why was I even alive? I wanted answers to these questions. I remembered back to when I was just ten years old, sitting at the kitchen table, and I asked Mom a lot of different fundamental questions, "I hear all these different churches on the radio, each saying they have the truth. I just don't understand what to believe."

Mother said, "I took you to the Unitarian Church because I wanted you to be able to choose what to believe."

I took on this freedom of choice as a heavy burden. As I lay in bed, my young brain swirled with all the religions asking, "Is this the TRUTH, or is this the WORD OF GOD?"

No one taught me to pray, but in Unitarian Sunday school we had a song. "Who can see the wind, neither you nor I, but when the trees bow down their heads, the wind is passing through." I loved the woods and the forest; I couldn't see God, but I felt God's presence in the beauty of nature. I prayed to that unseen presence, "Oh God, please tell me: what is the truth?" as I fell into a troubled sleep. My prayers went unanswered. I was looking for direction, for a voice to say, "This is the way", but I felt only static and confusion, alone in the world.

In eighth grade Sunday school, we went on field trips to other churches. The churches told us what they believed, but no one told me what was THE TRUTH. Some of the other students thought all these religions were silly; I just felt confused and; I wanted answers.

In ninth grade, we quit going to the Unitarian Church. Both of my brothers, Dennis and Eugene hated it, and Mother was tired of arguing and pushing them to go every Sunday morning.

My soul was grounded in confusion and my body was in the throes of a sexual change. Urges came and went with every breath. God seemed silent, out of reach.

Vivekananda said that Akasha is the infinite, omnipresent material of this universe, while Prana is the infinite, omnipresent manifesting power of this universe. Pranayama is learning to control Prana. But he warned - to really practice Yoga, one needed a guru, an enlightened teacher to guide one. I had no idea how to find a guru. The first step in Raja Yoga was to practice the five yamas: Ahimsa, non-violence; Satya, truthfulness; Asteya, non-stealing; Brahmacharya, chastity or marital fidelity; Aparigraha, non-possessiveness.

I decided to try to follow the first one, Ahimsa, and stopped eating meat. My mother noticed it first thing. "Why aren't you eating?"

"I don't want to eat meat. I don't want to kill anything."

Mother was sympathetic, "I don't like killing things either, but you need to eat complete protein. If you don't eat meat you will have to eat soybeans."

Soybeans? They sounded awful. I tried some, but I didn't know how to cook them. They tasted like squishy circles of dry sand. I decided to wait to study all this properly when a guru showed up. Vivekananda said that when the aspirant was ready, a guru would appear. I continued the breathing practice when the world seemed out of control, praying silently that someday my guru would arrive and lead me to the truth.

CHAPTER 2

First Job and First Love
1963-1965

IN MARCH 1963 Kennedy was president, and the world was full of hope. I turned 16 on March 17th. Now I could get a job, save for college, and get a room of my own.

My best friend Marie and I trudged through the snow towards Bridgeman's, the local ice cream parlor to get our after-school treat. As we walked past the Scholar Coffee House, I asked, "Did you see Bob Dylan when he played there?"

"Oh yes, a few times. Remember how Maury Bernstein, that folk music expert used to shake his head whenever anyone mentioned Dylan. He thought Dylan was awful with his croaking voice. I loved the way he could play the guitar and the harmonica at the same time when he was starting out."

"Bob Dylan is so cool, I just love his songs, I wish I'd seen him when he played there." I changed the subject, "How is Marvin Davidov doing? Did he go on another Freedom Ride?" My mind filled with images of the Freedom Riders risking their lives in the South sitting in cafes for equal rights. There were black students here. We weren't like down South. They could eat in any restaurant.

"He's leaving next week for another protest," Marie said as a gust of wind blew us through the door of Bridgeman's. It was so cold; we were the only customers getting ice cream cones. I waved at Reggie Anderson, the black clerk from Perine's bookstore. He was sitting with another black student drinking coffee, proof that we were different from those cafes in Birmingham Alabama. Marie and I got our cones and walked out into the fluttering snow licking ice cream and snowflakes together, hardly aware of the cold. We were tough Minnesota girls.

The next week the snow melted. I went back to Bridgeman's determined to apply for my dream job, serving ice cream and making sundaes. They were busy; every seat was filled. I hoped to see a "Help wanted" sign, but there wasn't one up. Instead of applying for a job I looked for a seat to order a sundae.

"You can sit here," said a friendly voice, sitting alone with a cup of coffee and a book.

It was the guy who had been sitting with Reggie last week. I sat down and smiled. His curly black hair was cut short to his head. His broad face was dark, not light-colored like Reggie's.

"I'm Jeremy Flinders. Are you a friend of Reggie's?" he asked.

"Reggie works at Perines. He's an artist. Mother often hires him to frame her paintings. I'm Pat. What are you reading?"

"I'm reading *The Fire Next Time* by James Baldwin. It just came out."

I picked up the book and opened it to the first story: *My Dungeon Shook: Letter to my Nephew on the One Hundredth Anniversary of the Emancipation* "That looks like a very interesting book."

"It's eye-opening. You should read it. Baldwin writes like a poet., What are you reading?"

"I'm reading *No Exit* by Albert Camus."

"What is it about?"

"Camus is a French existentialist. *No Exit* is a play about a hell where people can't get away from people they hate."

"That sounds miserable. Baldwin speaks of how and why we must get along and love one another." he said with a smile as the waitress came for my order.

I nodded my head in agreement, thinking of Martin Luther King's speech that I'd gone to hear with my mother.

"I'll have Revel Fudge ice cream with marshmallow topping." I said, my taste buds demanding an ultimate sugar high.

"I've never heard of that sundae."

"I made it up myself." I said, revealing my young age with my bubbling enthusiasm.

The waitress returned with a tall wavy sundae glass. The brown and white ice cream was swimming in marshmallow syrup topped with whipped cream and a cherry.

I picked up the tiny spoon with a long handle and carefully carved out a small bite. All those sweet calories slid down my throat without a worry about their impact on my slim young figure. I ate the whole thing and took my hard-earned babysitting money up to the cashier to pay for it. As I gave her the money I whispered, "Are they hiring anyone?"

"No, they don't need any help right now."

"Oh," I said, trying not to sound too disappointed. I needed a job now; I couldn't wait for a future opening.

For the next few weeks, I kept walking around the stores looking to see if anyone posted a "Help wanted" sign. If Reggie and Jeremy were having coffee I always stopped for a chat.

One day when I walked into the house, mother confronted me saying, "What are you doing hanging around with Negroes in Dinkytown?"

I stared at her, my heart racing. "Mother, what are you saying? Are you saying I can't sit and talk to some guys because of the color of their skin?"

"People will talk you know," she said, as she wrinkled her nose.

"You took me to hear Martin Luther King talk two years ago. I'll quote him directly, he dreamed of a time *When all God's children, black men and white men, Jews & gentiles, protestants, and Catholics will be able to join hands.* By men I assume he meant women too. I don't care what people think. I thought we were beyond that here in Minnesota; and you, I thought you were beyond that."

"I don't know what to do with you." Mother said shaking her head, worried I'd be ostracized.

I walked three steps to my bedroom area, I'd have slammed the door, but I couldn't because it wasn't really a door just a flimsy accordion piece of plastic.

The next morning, I went back to Dinkytown, more determined than ever to get a job. If I saw Reggie or Jeremy, I certainly would sit and talk with them. It would be my own personal sit-in. I walked down 4th street staring in every shop window. Maybe the Varsity Theater had an opening, but nothing was posted. Finally, I saw an ad in the window of The Tokyo, a tiny Japanese restaurant, just down the street from the theater.

Tokyo Restaurant Dinkytown 1960s

I'd never been in that restaurant, but I cautiously opened the door, and said I'd like to apply for the job.

Noreo, the owner, smiled and said, "You wait on tables, take orders, wash dishes?"

I said, "Yes I can," smiling from ear to ear with my dimples showing. My red hair, which had grown out long, was in a neat bun on top of my head. I was thin with a perfect figure and a ready smile. I was hired immediately.

The first day I arrived promptly at 4:30 pm. Noreo handed me an apron with a pocket on the left containing a receipt book and a pencil to write orders. On the right was a big empty pocket for tips. A bell tingled when the door opened and the first customers came in and sat down either at the counter if they were alone, or at one of the tables against the wall if they were with a friend. I hurried over to them with the one-page menu, trying to hide my racing heart behind a big smile. They knew what they wanted and didn't even look at the menu. Later I got to know the regular customers, I didn't bother with the menu, I'd just ask, "Do you want the curry today?"

Noreo's curry was a favorite with almost everyone. It wasn't hot Indian style but smooth and creamy, with a turmeric essence glowing out from the rice with shrimp or chicken. His secret ingredient was grated apple. It makes curry that is sweet and smooth. As I took the order into the kitchen, my nose filled with the lovely spices floating out the swinging kitchen door. As soon as the dish was done, Noreo called out "Curry", "Udon", or "Tempura", whatever was ready, I'd reach through the swinging door and take it to the customer's table.

Most of the customers were foreign students from Japan, Korea, or Taiwan, with a few Americans showing up every now and then. Eventually I could tell where they were from by listening to them talk. Chinese words sang in short musical tones like going up and down a scale; Korean, while still tonal had more syllables, Japanese was very multisyllabic, and the sounds seemed to rhyme like poetry. They all ate with chopsticks, but forks were available if you were a clumsy American. I came around with refills of water and green tea, smiling everywhere.

When the customers left, I cleared the table and placed my tips in the large empty pocket. By the end of the night my apron hung down on the right side from the weight of the quarters and dimes filling it up. By 7:30 most of the customers had come and gone, and by 8:00 the dishes were all done. Noreo asked me to sit down at the counter and he cooked a special dish for me. The curry was good, but my favorite was the shrimp tempura, which I ate with a fork because I'd never tried chopsticks. My mouth still waters remembering how the vegetables and shrimp crunched in my teeth then melted as they slid down my throat. After that I skipped the three blocks home, the tip coins jingling in my pocket.

I burst through the door to our apartment and dumped the coins out on the kitchen table in front of my mother and little brother. I counted each one, in just one night I'd made $15 in tips. It was a fortune; previously, I'd only made fifty cents an hour babysitting. I started scheming as I stared at the money and looked at the flimsy accordion door on the room I shared with my younger brother.

"Mom, I can make enough to pay the rent on the front room and still save for college. I'll just use my tips for the rent."

Mother smiled, "That might work, if you can really make that much in tips. After all, you might not get as much every night. I need that $30 to pay the taxes, so you can't get behind on the rent."

"I'd never just stay there without paying the rent; I know you need it." I assured her.

As soon as the room on the first floor opened up, I moved in. Finally, a door I could lock. Plus, the room had its own door to the front porch.

On November 22, 1963, at 1:00 p.m. I was sitting in French, my favorite class when an announcement came over the loudspeaker, "President Kennedy's been shot."

I took a deep breath and gasped, "No!", right out loud. All the other students gasped too. At 1:30 a second announcement said, "President Kennedy is dead". When classes changed, we went through the halls in silence. As soon as the day was over, I raced home and glued my eyes to the television. All programs were cancelled except for the news, and the news was only a repeat of sadness. Vice President Johnson took an oath on the plane. They replayed the shooting again and again. All Saturday I watched TV, and on Sunday I watched live as Jack Ruby killed Lee Harvey Oswald. Hope was dead, and we would never know who really killed him. I felt lost.

I was determined to do something to change this world. I quit going on any dates. Anyways, with studying, Yoga practice and work, I didn't have time. Mother was in a financial bind; she didn't have enough money from the rent to pay the taxes and mortgage on the rooming house. She didn't want to take me away from my high school during my senior year, so she let me stay in our apartment in the rooming house with my older brother while she took a job as a housekeeper in another town.

She hoped I was mature enough to handle this, but she worried about it. I have the letters that prove I thought I knew all the answers. I wrote:

Dear Mother,

Don't worry about me. This fall even if you were home, I would see very little of you. This is my schedule Tuesday-Friday:

5:00 a.m. Get up to study

8:00-3:00 School

3:15 Stop at home, study

4:30-8:30 Work at the Tokyo restaurant

8:45 Go home finish homework

10:30 Go to bed

On Monday Marie will take my shift at the Tokyo so I have a day off, go to the library, do my homework etc. With this schedule I don't see how I can possibly make meals for my brothers during the week. Beside all this I want very badly to try out for the plays, which will take all my spare time on Monday and before work Tuesday through Friday. I know with the positivity of having the ability to accomplish all things that I can do this, as long as I know that you are all right and not working your head off.

Love, Patsy

I was in training to be Superwoman, doing all the work. I got distracted at the restaurant by a guy. He called himself Mike, but his real name was Masayoshi. His clothes were casual and neat, his skin a beautiful olive color, and his eyes were small with a beautiful almond shape.

He came in towards the end of my shift and talked to me while I washed the dishes. Then at closing time he continued to stay. When I sat down to eat my tempura with a fork he came over and held my hand, gently showing me how to hold the chopsticks. It felt like sparks were flying from his hand to mine. He smelled of Brut cologne, just a splash. His English was excellent, and he was a graduate student in International Relations.

One day, Maysayoshi said, "Would you like to go to dinner at the Nankin Sunday evening?"

The Nankin was my favorite restaurant in downtown Minneapolis. I didn't ask Mother; as I'd always done in the past. She wasn't around anyway, so I just said "Yes".

When we got to the restaurant, we didn't just wait in line to get a seat, Masayoshi talked to the waiters, and got us a special seat upstairs; he had worked there when he first came to America. I stared at the menu and said, "I'll get shrimp tempura", feeling like I was still at the Tokyo. In the dark light of the balcony, I carefully picked up the shrimp with my chopsticks as I stared into his twinkling eyes. I nibbled carefully, savoring each little bite. He stared back at me, his eyes seeming like they were eating me up, in an exciting new way that I'd never felt before.

After dinner, he stopped the car in front of my house, but before I could open the door he reached over and kissed me. The kiss lunged into my soul and charged my core, taking my breath away. Those urges were back, but this time, I didn't want to control them. I opened the car door and slowly walked into my room through my private front door feeling my mouth glowing from the warmth of his kiss.

We went on several other dates. My brothers noticed Masayoshi coming and picking me up with his car. They told Mother I was dating this older foreign student, and she forbade me to see him. I was disgusted - what right did they have to tell mother?

I was sure I knew everything. I wrote to her:

Dear Mother,

Before you get upset over what I have to say I want to tell you that I agree with you. I will stop going out now completely, but first I want to get a few things about myself and my ideals across to you so that you will perhaps understand me better. First if I ever go on any dates at all it will be with what you call a man. I am a virgin who knows how to take care of herself with any man. Some of the boys that I've known nowadays are worse than any man I've ever gone out with. So please, Mother, don't tell me about men and boys.

In a very few years I will be a foreign student myself and I hope that people will not be afraid to associate with me because of what people think! I have already been ostracized more when I was in eighth grade, than I will ever be again. To be honest I have very few friends in high school, and those which I would want would not condemn me for dating a Japanese man. You may think I'm young, but I don't know when I will be any older or more set on my social ideals. I had already decided to stop going out on dates before you came down here, but I found it very hard with you gone.

I stopped dating Masayoshi last week. But the outside pressures to have a male companion are horrible - the radio, friends, everybody thinks a person has to have somebody.

Love,

Patsy

She was in Lake Wilson, and my brothers really didn't know my schedule. Masayoshi kept courting me, so I relented on my promise to Mother. I did not practice Satya or truthfulness.

It was his mouth, the way his smile lifted his cheeks, and his twinkling eyes pulled me in that led me to believe every word he said. We both dreamed of a world at peace, in which everyone was treated with respect. We both even liked classical music. I started to see him on a regular basis but told my mother and my brothers that I wasn't. Even though Mother had an uncanny way of knowing if someone was lying, I found if I believed my lie, she couldn't tell I was lying.

WWII had ended 19 years ago, two years before I was born, but Masayoshi was eight years old when the war ended, and he remembered it. He was Japanese and his roommates were Korean but spoke Japanese; they had been forced to learn it during the occupation. Masayoshi and his roommates' parents had probably been enemies. My parents had worked in the war effort against Japan, but now Japan and America were friends. Masayoshi and I and his roommates too, wanted to forge a new world order, one of Peace and Love.

One day as I stepped out of Masayoshi's car an older Caucasian man who rented the apartment below him stepped out the door. He glared at me. I felt he'd like to have us both tarred and feathered. I glared back, defiant, and threw back my long red hair as I marched up the stairs arm in arm with Masayoshi. Perhaps he had fought in that terrible war, but now times had changed.

We spent every free moment together. Steeped in the ideals of love and marriage, I pretended we got married in his bedroom to the last lines from *West Side Story,* "Somewhere" before I lost my virginity. We stood together next to the bed, and I sang the words that Maria sang before she made love to Tony. "A time and place for us. Hold my hand and we're halfway there. Hold my hand and I'll take you there. Somehow, someday, somewhere." In this way I practiced my version of Brahmacharya (chastity).

We kissed, absorbing each other's essence. We wiggled out of our clothes in his small bedroom. I lay naked on his single bed in the apartment he shared with his roommates who weren't home. He caressed me all over, working my body into a frenzy. My body rose up to meet him, opening, accepting all he had to give. Suddenly he sat up and deftly put on a condom. He entered me slowly, and gently, there was no pain, only a unity, a warmth, a oneness as our bodies pulsed together. As we calmed, we noticed a small amount of blood on the sheets that proved I had indeed been a virgin. I didn't need to control these sensual urges anymore; I could just go with the flow, sharing these sensations with Masayoshi, my perfect lover.

A few weeks later I was sitting next to Masayoshi in his car, and we were driving across the 10th Avenue Bridge. We passed a large Buick car going in the opposite direction. The driver turned and stared at me. It was MOM. *What was she doing here?* I thought she was at her job in Lake Wilson. I tried to duck down on the floor, but it was too late, I knew she'd seen me. The game was up, my heart sunk.

Mom had come home to check on things. She pulled into the driveway shortly after Masayoshi dropped me off. "How could you! I trusted you and you lied to me." As she yelled, her eyes glowed and the veins on her forehead popped out.

My body tensed, wanting to run away from her glare. "I'm sorry Mom, but I just couldn't stop seeing him. I love him, and he loves me."

"Well, you'd better stop seeing him," she said, those glaring eyes staring at me, yet again.

My head shook, my heart slumped. How could I disappoint her so. She had trusted me, let me stay here on my own. I loved her, I wanted to please her. A boyfriend wasn't that important.

I told Masayoshi over the telephone, "We'll just have to break up." Trying to keep my voice calm, as I held back tears.

He said, "No I will talk to your mother."

When I told Mom that he wanted to see her, she was surprised. "He'd better have something good to say for himself," she scoffed. He came to our little apartment all dressed up in a nice sweater and dress slacks. His eyes twinkled with that undeniable smile.

"I love your daughter, and I'd like to marry her someday. I know she is young, but she is wonderful to me. I know she needs to finish school, but I will wait for her. If you refuse to allow me to continue to see her, I will not do so, and we will both be very sad."

His English was as impeccable as his manners. She was impressed. She let us continue to see each other. After she went back to her job at Lake Wilson, I felt guilty and wrote her a letter with an explanation of why I'd disobeyed her.

Dear Mother,
Even if at times it hurts you, I am such a stubborn little idiot that I have to think things out for myself, even though you tell me not to do them.

For the first time in my life I had met someone whose ideals were like mine and whom I truly admired. I was so selfish that I could not bring myself to give him up, nor could I give up my ambitions. I could almost compare my position with that of my grandmother 90 years ago, because Mike can actually be compared to your father. Because he was 10 years older than your mother. But today is not 90 years ago. Times have changed and the position of women in society has changed. I have to take the hard way, my own way, and have the courage to learn things for myself. I had to think this out for myself. I couldn't just drop into the gutter someone whom I admired so, and whom I loved to be with, and who seemed to understand and admire me in return. I couldn't leave him because he was so many years older than I, nor because you said so, when you didn't even know the whole situation, and I did not know how to tell you. I fought this more with myself than with him or you because he said it was all up to me and if I really was sure I didn't want to see him anymore, he would certainly comply.

I am never alone, nor will I ever be alone. In fact, I now feel that being alone is much more restrictive than if you have a good partner. A partner who does not grasp, but holds your hand and shares his experiences as you share your experiences Such a partner will never be a restriction.

I am young, but I know what I want. I have found a partner who is much older than I, but he can learn from my youth as I can learn from his age and experience. I did not fall in love with him, but I am growing in love for him every day, a love which I want to continue for my entire life.

Marriage for me is not a way out, nor a way in, nor an easy way, nor the end. I do not want "to get married", but I want to be with the man I love. I want to marry him - live with him, study with him, travel with him, and eventually raise his children.

Love,

Patsy

So, I spent all my free time during my senior year with Masayoshi, mostly in his bed, with all those high ideals. He was a very good lover, and I reveled in every minute.

I didn't attend the all-night party for seniors; I was just too grown-up for that. I didn't wait for Freshman orientation at the University. I started college in summer school right after graduation. I was buried in more assignments than I'd ever imagined possible.

Masayoshi started working full-time for Kodak and went on a trip to New York. I was overwhelmed by my classes and lost without Masayoshi. When he returned, he called me and said, "I don't want to see you anymore, you've been unfaithful."

I couldn't believe my ears. "What do you mean?"

"When I was gone, my sister, invited you over and then you went out with her friend," he said.

"He invited me to see a movie. It was nothing. I wasn't unfaithful. I didn't even really want to go, but they said it was just as a friend, not a date, I said, "Come over; we need to talk," feeling sure if he saw me, he would understand.

We went for a walk, and he told me the truth, "Well maybe you weren't unfaithful, but I was unfaithful to you."

I was shocked, I just couldn't believe it. Why would he do that? I thought we were in LOVE. He walked me back home, and I never saw him again. At work, I'd stare out the window at the restaurant looking for him, but he never came.

Mother had returned from her job out of town. As soon as my classes were over, I realized Masayoshi really wasn't coming back. I went to bed and refused to get up. Mother brought meals to my room. I just stayed there; my heart broken in two; scattered on the floor. It was only my breath that made the covers move. I didn't know how I'd ever face the world alone.

Thirty-three years later, after the death of my mother, I found my letters that I'd written to her. She saved them all. She never said, "I told you so." Letters are a treasure, that is fast disappearing from the world.

Travel and the internet in the 21st century allowed me to reconnect with Masayoshi. Over fifty years after he'd left, I still wanted to know why, so when I was visiting friends in Tokyo, I looked him up. We met in the elevator, instantly recognizing each other on our way to the designated rendezvous. Over dinner, I wanted to tell him what an asshole he was and find out why he'd left me.

He said, "I just thought you were too young." A crappy excuse for breaking a young woman's heart.

But after he told me about his life, I was happy he hadn't married me. I wasn't ready to be grown up at 18. I just had to thank him for teaching me and leaving. He'd had his life's journey, and I had mine.

CHAPTER 3

Finding a True Husband
1965-1968

I'D STARTED COLLEGE at the University of Minnesota in summer school because I was in a hurry to grow up. I thought I was so smart. I discovered in that first summer session that I didn't know much, not about men nor anything else. The university was not year 13 of high school. I got the first and last D in my life in French, the class I did so well in during high school. It was a slap in the face, that woke me up. I was only 18, so in the fall I signed up for Freshman orientation at the University of Minnesota. I needed any help I could get.

I met my husband that freshman year in geology lab. The lab was held in an Quonset hut left over from WWII called, Temporary North of Folwell. I remembered walking in, the first day. The floor jiggled like a trampoline as I walked around, and the air was musty smelling. I sat down next to a pretty brunette girl. All the students sat in pairs. Each pair of students had to carry a heavy tray of rocks to our seats from a cupboard. At the end of class, I looked at my lab partner and said, "Next time, let's sit with guys, and they can carry the rocks." There were lots of guys in the room with strong upper bodies.

I stood in the doorway at the beginning of the next class, looking for an empty seat next to a guy. Still on a rebound from my dark-haired lover, I was attracted to dark-haired guys, but they were all taken. The only one with an empty seat was a very skinny blond, not much to look at from the distance.

As I sat down, I got a close-up view. His face was a Scandinavian marvel. He had high cheekbones, and twinkling bright blue eyes placed in deep sockets under carefully carved eyebrows. *Maybe he's blond, but he is cute*, I thought. *Besides, I'm sure he'll carry the rocks.*

He glanced at me with deep-set blue eyes and made a face more like a grimace than a smile. But I smiled back and said, "Hi, I'm Pat."

Forced to reply, he finally smiled and said, "I'm Bob."

He carried the rocks without complaining. I loved the way he examined them. Together we scratched for hardness, looked through a magnifying glass and sniffed the rocks. But I spent the time looking at him more than at the rocks. His shyness attracted me, I wanted to learn more about him.

The next lab we sat together again. This time he smiled as he carried the rocks. Later he admitted his first thought when I sat down next to him the first day was "Damn, now I've got to carry the rocks both ways."

After that second class, as we left the building, I tossed my long scarf around my face purposely letting it hit Bob on the shoulder. He grabbed one end of it. A cold wind turned my face red, and my long hair blew out behind me. I laughed and tugged at my end of the scarf as he held on tight to his end. We played tug-of-war right outside the classroom door. We didn't even see the other students going out of their way to walk around us. I thought, *This is fun, Masayoshi refused to even run down a hill with me, let alone play.* I invited Bob over to my place after the next class to listen to classical music. I thought, *I bet I can teach him a thing or two.*

Bob was a joy to be around. He listened to everything I had to say and every idea I had. He'd never had a girlfriend before, so I got to teach him everything I'd learned from Masayoshi about sex. His lack of sexual experience was more than compensated for by his adoration and youthful energy. Just rubbing our bodies together completely clothed could induce an orgasm for us both.

Intellectually we were both interested in everything. We were devoted to the ideal of peace and making the world a better place for everyone. In addition, we were almost the same age, and from the same country, or so I thought. When he brought me over to meet his parents, they were stiff and nervous, and spoke with a slight accent. Bob explained they were Finnish Americans, and he'd spoken Finnish until he was five years old.

Just before Christmas of that Freshman year, Bob sat me on his lap and said, "Will you marry me? I want to take care of you for the rest of my life. I'll never leave you."

I knew he meant it with all his heart. I wasn't so sure about myself. I was still rebounding from Masayoshi, but he felt like the rock I needed to lean on. After being rejected by my first lover myself, I couldn't think of rejecting his love. I said "Yes." And we were engaged.

Shortly after I said yes, I got an unexpected phone call.

"Hi, this is Jeremy. Remember me? We used to talk at Bridgeman's."

"Sure, I remember you." I said softly wondering why he'd called and how he'd gotten my phone number.

"You were too young for me to ask then, but I know you're old enough now. How'd you like to go out?" he asked.

"Mm, I really can't" I said, my mind spinning to find some nice words. I never had thought of him as a boyfriend, just a friend. I certainly wasn't interested in having anything to do with an older man. Besides I was safe, I was engaged.

"Why not?" he asked his voice taking on a demanding tone.

"Thanks for thinking of me, but I'm engaged to a very nice, honest young man who loves me very much. He's never been hurt, and I wouldn't want to hurt him."

He didn't say congratulations or anything nice like that, he just said, "Oh, you will hurt him one day. I can guarantee that."

"You are entirely wrong," I said and hung up the phone, shaking. *Why did he say that?* I wondered.

I wanted to love and honor Bob for the rest of my life. We shared a vision of the world at peace, not the war we saw around us as more young men were being drafted into the Vietnam War. We read **Stranger in a Strange Land** and shared the main character's idea that we might grok one another and reach an understanding so complete that we merged with each other becoming one in mind, body and spirit. Together we became lacto-vegetarians, not wanting to cause harm to any living creature. I followed the suggestions from **Diet for a Small Planet** to create meals with complete proteins.

Nobody was a vegetarian back then, but Bob embraced it with the same intensity that he had embraced me. Bob said, "I remember the chickens running around with their heads cut off on the farm. I don't want to inflict that pain on any other creature." We were engaged on our own path to live true to our ideals. Peace for the world, and at peace with what we needed to consume for our survival.

One evening Bob came over to my place, his eyes were sparkling with excitement. He said, "I want you to try something. I think you'll like it."

"What is it?" I asked, surprised by the glow in Bob's eyes.

"You'll see, you've just got to try it." We went to the West Bank Campus; the area was being renovated and there were empty storefronts. We went in through the back door of an abandoned building. The only light came from streetlights shining in from the outside. "I want you to meet Jimmy. He just came from California."

I turned and shook hands with a skinny young man who didn't stop moving as he smiled and said, with a broad smile, "So you want to try some weed?"

"I...I...', stumbling over my words, looking at Bob.

"Oh, just try it. It'll open your mind," Bob said, answering for me.

"Take a seat." Jimmy said, waving towards the old barber's chair in the center of the room.

I climbed up into the chair as Jimmy pulled out a skinny cigarette.

"I don't smoke," I said, staring at the skinny rolled paper balanced between his fingers.

"You don't smoke it. You just breathe in a puff," he explained as he lit it and loudly sucked in a big hit. Bob took a hit and passed it to me.

"Mmm, okay I'll try it," I said, still hesitating, staring at the smelly weed burning between my fingers. I pressed my lips around the burning stick and took a deep breath in.

As the smoke entered my lungs, I immediately felt relaxed. All my worries vanished. I just felt present in the sensations of the moment. Jimmy leaned the barber chair back and spun it around. I giggled. My mind didn't feel opened, but it was totally relaxed. I felt like smiling until my cheeks started to ache. After that we smoked pot almost every weekend except when work got in the way. Despite smoking dope, I kept up a B+ average and Bob also continued to get good grades.

The February before our marriage two years later, we'd filled out an application to work as lookouts for the forest service. Bob's ambition was to be a forest ranger working for the Park Service. He'd gone to Yellowstone with his family as a boy and had dreamed of being there again ever since. We weren't married yet, but the wedding date was set. We jumped up and down when we were hired to man a lookout tower in the Absaroka Primitive area just outside of Yellowstone National Park

In April, while attending forestry camp up north, Bob bought an old International truck. He rebuilt the engine and made the rear compartment into a camper van for us.

We wrote our own wedding vows, promising to be married for all eternity, not just till death do us part. Dr. Foot, the Unitarian minister, having more experience with life, advised against those words, but didn't make us change. We thought our vows might take a long time, but didn't practice them, or time them. They only took 10 minutes. My aunt made banana bread for refreshments. We drank apple juice and opened a few presents at the church with about 20 friends and relatives.

We spent our wedding night - June 8, 1967 - sleeping on the floor of a friend's apartment. Our friends all got high, and we just held onto each other, now we were legally one. The next day we left behind all the dope and parties and headed out in the van towards the Rocky Mountains.

Standing in front of our International Truck,
ready to leave for the Absaroka Primitive Area

We were headed to our dream job in the Absaroka Primitive Area in Montana. We didn't need to smoke any grass; we were high on nature, as we camped along the way. After a week we arrived in the town of Gardiner, Montana, with only $10.00 left for expenses. We thought we'd be going up to the tower right away, but we had to stay in town for the first month because the trail to the tower was still covered in snow.

When we checked in at the office, they told Bob he had to get a haircut before they'd give us a charge account at the grocery store. Bob's hair was just beginning to touch his neck, but they said they didn't want any hippies working for the Forest Service. Since the tower wasn't open yet, Bob was sent out to help the trail crew.

After work he dragged himself into the motel room and lay down on the bed. His face looked like tanned ash, while his blond hair gleamed whiter than ever. I fixed dinner and brought it to him in bed. Bob said, "We were using a pulaski (a tool with an ax on one end and a hoe on the other) to grub out weed trees at 8,000 feet."

Bob and I grew up at an elevation of just 600 feet, so working at that high elevation was exhausting. In addition to that, we discovered years later that he had a heart defect. I stayed in our motel, did sketches, and went hiking. There wasn't any work for me until we got to the tower. Women did not work with the trail crew in those days. I didn't mind, I knew I wasn't strong enough to handle a pulaski.

Friday at the end of Bob's first week we went out to the local bar and hung out with the trail crew. As we sat holding hands, Lefty, from the trail crew said, "You two look like newlyweds."

I giggled and said, "Yes, we just got married June 8th."

They were all eating chicken wings, but Bob declined, saying, "We're vegetarians and don't want to kill other living things." They stared at us in shock, as if we were from another planet.

On July 19th the trails were clear, and we mounted horses for a two-day ride into the wilderness to get to the tower on Lookout Mountain. Although we'd had a horse on the farm when I was a little girl, I'd never ridden one before. We rode up and down countless hills and forded two mountain streams clean enough to drink from.

We finally stopped at 6:30 pm. My butt hurt, and I was suffering from motion sickness. The assistant ranger admitted that he refused to ride my horse because his gait was so rough, especially going downhill. They'd had me ride him because he was small. We stopped overnight at Buffalo Station, an empty isolated cabin on the trail. I was too ill to eat or help with dinner, but I did make breakfast the next morning and then we proceeded up the mountain, 2,000 more feet. The trail wound up and around towering pines. We were dwarfed by their presence; their beauty numbed me to the pain in my butt.

Finally, we saw our destination - a small square structure balanced on the edge of a 10,000-foot cliff overhead. I craned my neck to look up. It didn't look like this sketch yet; the flag wasn't up, and the windows were all boarded up. When we arrived, the crew helped us make it look like the sketch. They lifted the hinged boards covering the windows. The boards braced at a 90-degree angle became a roof over the walkway around the glassed-in tower. We found the flag and hoisted it up the flagpole.

Our job was to go out on the balcony of the tower and scan the forest every hour with binoculars, checking for fires. Every morning we checked in via short wave radio, and every two weeks the road crew came via horseback and brought us supplies.

During lightning storms, we were high enough to be right in the middle of a storm cloud. I loved laying on the foam mattress watching the 360-degree light show through the glass windows. We were instructed to stay on the foam mattress of the bed in case lightning entered the cabin. We had a lightning rod, to ground the cabin, but they had told us stories of balls of lightning bouncing off the iron stove. I was too young to be afraid, I even hoped maybe I'd get to see a lightning ball roll across the floor. I did worry when Bob got up from the mattress to plot where the lightning struck with the metal plotter. As soon as he finished, I'd grab his hand and pulled him back down on the mattress with me. The next morning, we checked all the spots we'd plotted for fires. One morning after a storm we did spot a fire starting. The fire crew came with an airplane and dropped water on the flames, stopping it before it became a forest fire. Bob spent his spare time developing a better map for plotting those lightning strikes.

My Indian ink drawing of the lookout tower

The best evenings were when the lightning stayed far away, and we could watch the show from our home in the clouds. For fun we made up our own name for this far away lightning - we called it "kawambi".

Every morning, being the earlier riser, I started a fire in the wood-burning stove. Then I walked up the mountain and picked a bouquet of purple mountain lupine. The lupine covered the mountain top with low-lying purple-white stalks of color. In the bouquet they flowed over the edges of a small bowl perched on our little breakfast table squeezed in across the stove.

To wash our clothes, every week I built a fire and heated water melted from a glacier.

Heating water and washing clothes the old-fashioned way

Each simple act of living here made life slow down and become real. Each day had its own calm rhythm at one with nature, living on the edge of the sky. No machines, no cars, no stereo, no radio except for that short wave radio that we used to check in with the ranger station. Occasionally the peace would be broken by an Air Force plane breaking the sound barrier over our heads. The loud bang felt like my ear drums would burst, shattering the quiet of the mountain.

Bob had to carry water up hill on his back from that glacier run-off. This wasn't easy, his forehead would be dripping with perspiration when he finally got the tank up the steps into the tower. We tried to use as little water as possible. We took our baths by warming water down at the glacier run off where I washed clothes.

A rare tourist came and took a picture of us in front of the sign we'd made with the tower behind us. We hadn't thought of taking pictures of ourselves at all. This became one of our treasured memories.

The trail crew came to get us when the first snow started to fall on September 1st. "Stop in the office tomorrow to get your review. It's been nice knowing you," the crew chief said as he dropped us off at our motel room.

"It's been nice knowing you, too," we replied, sad to have this magical summer come to an end.

We'd gotten along well with everyone, and Bob even did an extra project to make charting lightning strikes easier for the next crew, so we weren't worried about our review. As we walked into the office, we were confronted by a very grim face instead of the usual smile. Without saying a word our boss handed us our review. As we started to read it, he said, "First of all we found out that you lied on your application."

We both looked at him in shock, then remembered we'd said we were already married, not that we were getting married June 8th.

Then, reading on, the report said that Bob was "lazy". Neither of us could believe this. Yes, he'd gotten tired and out of breath when he worked on the trail at first with the pulaski, but "lazy"? We just stared at him.

"You know you guys just wouldn't be good working for the Forest Service. You're vegetarians and no one would understand that. You should just do research."

"We don't make judgements about other people. We are not opposed to people hunting," Bob said, but the boss just shook his head. His mouth stayed in a grim straight line; nothing would change his mind.

We were devastated. We walked out of the office, grabbed our things and started driving home. We drove continuously day and night, not stopping to sleep anywhere. As he drove angry and hurt, Bob kept muttering under his breath, "How are we ever going to work for the Forest Service with a review like that? Research, it's just crap, I want to be out in the field."

Tears welled up in my eyes but didn't flow down my cheeks as I clenched my teeth, trying to stay awake, and keep Bob awake. I was afraid Bob would get into a crash as we drove on, and on.

We discovered after we returned home from our job, that lots of our friends had been arrested for possession of marijuana. We took our pipes and hid them in the attic of Bob's parents' house, worried that we too would be arrested.

It seemed the universe had closed on us, and we were looking for new directions. Timothy Leary's book *The Psychedelic Experience* had just come out recently. All our friends were reading it. We didn't read the book, but we wanted the knowledge LSD was said to provide. Bob had friends who were graduate students in chemistry. They offered him some LSD tabs and he brought them home for us to try. We reasoned, it's legal, the universe is closed, so why not open our minds with LSD.

I remember that first trip. I stared at the postage stamp-sized stain on a piece of paper. It seemed like there was nothing there, just some crystals on the paper. I licked it, an acid taste filled my mouth. Then I panicked *What are we doing? We don't know what this is. Maybe its poison.* "Let's vomit it up. Don't raw eggs make people vomit?" I asked.

Bob just nodded his head in agreement.

I grabbed two raw eggs and carefully broke them into two plates. We sat down at the table facing the eggs. As I picked up my fork and approached the egg, it slid across the plate, running away from the fork. We were going on this trip, like it or not. Bob and I lay down in bed together, our heads spinning out of control for the next twelve hours. I spiraled down into a hole, colors of the universe spinning around me. My eyes beheld a new world. Everything seemed to vibrate like it was alive. As I stared at my potted geranium its vibrations blended with my own, just a bit closer than inanimate objects. Then when I touched Bob's arm, a spark of the life force flowed between us, binding us together. Thoughts and images of past experiences flowed through my mind: my whole life went by in a flash; everyone and everything was one. As we came out of this high, we thought Timothy Leary is right - if everyone dropped acid maybe there wouldn't be war.

We dropped acid some more, and weekends lasted forever, staying awake the whole time. A typical acid trip can last 6 to 15 hours. It didn't leave much time for recovery (which can take 24 hours) doing our college assignments or getting the housework done. Subsequent trips seemed like a repeat, then repeat again. They lost their appeal. The next year after LSD became illegal, an old acquaintance of Bob's who was now in the police academy stopped by and said, "We got some acid from a raid. Wow, did we ever have a trip. We were out at the cabin with some other police cadets, and we had a ball shooting frogs. You should have seen the blood fly in multiple colors."

My stomach wanted to turn inside out - LSD just made them violent, not peaceful. It was all an illusion. I wanted more than a passing trip, so I quit all drugs and got serious about studying Yoga, lucky that I hadn't gotten some bad stuff and blown my brains out. Bob quit grass and LSD too. Instead, he started to hang out at the Triangle Bar on the West Bank of the university. He said he had to go there to play pool. I'd go along and sketch and drink water. I even made pizza at home and delivered it to him in the bar.

Bob said, "Let's have a Halloween Party. I'll get a keg and invite all our friends."

I loved Halloween. The old duplex we rented was perfect for a Halloween party. It had a large open room on the first floor, with a bay window full of plants. I'd made a God's Eye cover for the ceiling light out of yarn and grape vines, so even the upstairs was eerie, but the cellar was scary. It had a dirt floor, with rough stone walls covered with real spider webs. There was a small alcove in the wall big enough for me to sit in meditation.

I made food and set it out. I dressed in my costume, all black with tights and a witch's hat. I descended into the cellar and climbed up into the alcove. I spent the entire evening there with my legs crossed in meditation. I heard the noise of the party, and let it be far away. I didn't need to talk to anyone. I didn't need to pretend to drink or smoke. If the guests wanted to see me, they had to go into the cellar, but I didn't talk to anyone, I was very happy playing a hermit witch.

CHAPTER 4

Finding a Career and Looking for a Guru

1968-1970

I RUSHED THROUGH COLLEGE finishing in three years with an honors degree in Japanese; it was cheaper that way. I decided if we couldn't join the Peace Corps or the Forest Service, at least with my liberal arts degree in Japanese, I would land a good job. I didn't want to end up like my mother, a widow with no way of earning a living.

It was 1968, the time of the Great Society, and there were lots of opportunities for new liberal arts graduates. Companies came to interview students at the university, and I arrived armed with my honors degree expecting to be interviewed for an international job. I approached the desk and was greeted with this statement. "Nobody wants to interview women, except the telephone company."

I was speechless. Nobody had ever said that to me before. *All that work going to college, getting a degree, but only men get to be interviewed?* My mind raced, I wanted an interesting job; I couldn't imagine myself at the phone company bossing around a pile of women telephone operators. I gathered up my papers and quickly walked out the door, resisting an urge to slam it behind me.

The school was holding hearings about the placement office, and how it was being used to support the war effort. I decided to testify about these companies not interviewing women. I told them how I felt just as qualified as any of the men that were being interviewed. They said, "These hearings are about the war, *not women*."

I felt ashamed to bring this up when young men were being killed in Vietnam. Bob faced the draft too. He was on a student deferment. Following the ideals of ahimsa, (non-violence) Bob applied to be a conscientious objector in 1966, but he could still be drafted.

I left the placement office and wandered around campus totally rejected, just because I was a woman. Bob was still working on his degree, so I needed a job. I walked by a table in the hall of the Coffman Memorial Union, the student union building on the east side of campus. A smiling young woman sat behind the table with a sign: "The Teacher Corps." I would have loved to be in the Peace Corps but that seemed out of the question. I approached the desk with the sign, "What is it?" I asked.

"We're looking for liberal arts graduates who'd like to teach junior high in the inner city."

"That's me," I said, and picked up their application. I wasn't sure that was what I wanted, but it sounded much better than working for the telephone company, ordering some women around. I filled out the form, making up a story about liking junior high, and a month later I received the notice that I'd been accepted. I spent two years as an intern in the Minneapolis public schools, teaching and studying art with a wonderful group of students recruited from around the United States. After I finished that program, there weren't any jobs for art teachers in Minneapolis. Again, I searched for a new direction. I'd really enjoyed working in small groups with kids that had behavioral problems in an alternative school program, to me they were creative and fun, not problems. I applied for and received a scholarship to be trained as a special education teacher, majoring in educational psychology and reading instruction.

My goal was to work with children who had emotional and behavioral problems. I remembered how finding Yoga had helped me as a teenager, so I thought in addition to my graduate studies, I could find a Yoga teacher. As an undergraduate I had tried to find a Yoga teacher by studying Sanskrit. Sanskrit was the ancient language of Yoga. I had read in Vivekananda's book that some concepts could only be said in Sanskrit. Dharma is a philosophical terminology for both ethics & metaphysics; it is neither scientific nor political. "Om" is the sound of a sacred Sanskrit symbol of the ultimate reality. They do not exist in English.

I remembered that first day in Sanskrit class. I was in awe of the instructor Dr. Usharbudh Arya, a broad-shouldered man from India with curly black hair that framed his head like a halo. He greeted us, smiling, and bowing his head.

He looked uncomfortable in western clothes. As he stood at the chalkboard, lips moved silently as they repeated the sacred texts and then he picked up the chalk and wrote them for us in English. I was mesmerized.

Dr. Arya, a Brahmin, had been a child prodigy. He learned ancient texts as a child and had traveled, giving lectures, when he was very young. His wife hadn't come to America yet and he was living in student housing. He invited the Sanskrit class over to his apartment and taught us how to make authentic vegetarian curry. First, he carefully melted butter in a frying pan; as it heated up solids came bubbling to the surface, which he carefully removed. "This is how you make ghee or clarified butter; see how clear it is when it is finished," he said.

I watched carefully as he ground up whole pickling spices into a fresh curry powder using a blender. "The secret is to grind your spices fresh, and then to fry them in ghee before you add anything else," he said. He placed the spices into the hot ghee; the room filled with the fresh essence of curry spice. Then he added the dahl, (soaked lentils). As they cooked, he rolled out whole wheat dough and heated it over an open flame until it bubbled. We used the bread to scoop up the delicious curry, making a vegetarian meal much tastier than the soybean burgers I'd been making for Bob.

Sanskrit proved to be an almost impossible language for me; not only did it have a different alphabet, but it didn't even separate the words. You were supposed to be able to tell where a word ended by the ending put on it. I still wanted to study yoga. "Please, you know so much. Couldn't you teach us yoga?" I asked Dr Arya.

"No, I'm not worthy, I don't have a guru," was his answer to me and others who asked him. I didn't understand why he insisted that he couldn't teach us.

One day when Arya was teaching Sanskrit, he received a call from someone who spoke to him in Sanskrit. The call had come from Swami Rama. Swami Rama was at Menninger Research Institute in Topeka, Kansas. There Dr. Elmer Green was doing experiments on him that proved, through the practice of yoga, he could control his autonomic nervous system and even stop his heartbeat. Swami Rama came to Minneapolis and met with Dr Arya. He gave him an initiation that Dr Arya said totally opened his mind to the universe. After that, Dr. Arya became a dedicated disciple of Swami Rama.

When I returned to the University on my scholarship, I contacted Dr. Arya about finding a Yoga teacher. I was surprised when he said, "I'm so glad you called. I found a guru and I'm teaching raja yoga; you can join us if you'd like."

At least twice a week, I walked through the quiet tree-lined streets and ascended three flights to the meditation temple we helped Dr. Arya create in his attic. I sat cross-legged on the floor with the other students. I learned to relax through prana, breath awareness. My mind calmed to a state of joy where any use of mind-altering chemicals was unnecessary. As we chanted together, I felt an intense sense of belonging, being one in the present.

The group gathering grew to include not just students but professors from the university who wanted to study yoga. We were studying raja yoga; it is a discipline of mind and body control that focuses on meditation. According to this discipline the biggest obstacle to self-realization is a busy mind. A thinking ego, craving, and attachment contribute to suffering on earth. The suffering was a continuous cycle of birth and rebirth that could end only if one attained enlightenment. I remembered from when I studied Vivekananda's book in ninth grade, that raja yoga was the royal path, the true way to enlightenment. Arya lectured us on the proper steps to follow in studying yoga.

"If you want to study yoga you must not use any mind-altering substances. You must practice truthfulness and non-violence."

I started waking up early to meditate, at least half an hour before Bob. I started my day sitting cross-legged in the closet, clearing my mind and attaining a high without drugs. Arya lectured us on the importance of receiving a mantra.

"Each mantra is chosen for the disciple based on their personality. Your mantra will consist of a combination of syllables for the release of specific energies through constant repetition and meditation. The mantra will stay in your mind forever. Often it comes to the surface of the mind without conscious invitation. Even when the initiate is not consciously aware of his mantra, it is there helping to raise his consciousness. THERE IS NO MEDITATION WITHOUT A MANTRA."

I was honored to be one of the first students that Arya initiated with a mantra. This was the first initiation in yoga. He touched my forehead as I sat on the floor, my mind in a calm meditative state, and whispered my secret Sanskrit words in my ear. "Aim Harim, Cleme Nama Shiva ya." I repeated them constantly, silently in my mind, concentrating on my breath, breathing in the mantra, and breathing it out. Even while I was driving or walking around, I repeated those words in my mind. It was like being in a constant state of awareness. *Aim Harim, Cleme Nama Shiva ya* over and over in my mind, but not out loud. I was never to say them aloud.

Arya said, "If you receive a mantra initiation you can count on life-long guidance and help. The science of meditation has no end (until total liberation is reached); there are always higher steps to take. The initiator is responsible for the initiate's spiritual progress, irrespective of any other consideration. It is a life-long relationship."

Practicing yoga was a dream come true. I'd found a teacher. Maybe soon the time would be ready, and I would find an enlightened guru. Arya was like a father to me, he even said it would be a lifelong relationship. I trusted him. I trusted his advice. My trust for Dr Arya reminded me how much I'd adored my own father.

Arya told us about Swami Rama. He was enlightened and knew our past and our future. He was beyond the earthly realm. Arya told us that one's relationship with one's guru was such that if he said jump off a cliff, you did so without hesitation. The enlightened guru was beyond morals, beyond right and wrong, so did no wrong. Swami-ji (Swami Rama) had been a Shankaracharya, (which he explained as being a sort of Hindu pope in a part of India). Arya told a weird story that a dying businessman offered Swami Rama his body, so Swami Rama transferred his being into the businessman's body and continued to live, while the body of the Shankaracharya was dead and disposed of. I dismissed this story as myth, but I was impressed by the research that had been done on him. People believed Swami Rama did healing miracles, and he had shown that he could stop his heart from beating or, at least in a meditative state, put his heart into arterial fibrillation in experiments at the Menninger Research Foundation.

I received training on how to initiate other members and give them a mantra. I was very good at practicing progressive relaxation and doing guided meditation for a large group of people.

One day we were honored by Swami Rama visiting us in Dr. Arya's attic "temple". Before he arrived, Dr. Arya said, "Remember that you are in the presence of an enlightened soul. Be sure to bow your head when you approach him."

I remember sitting cross-legged on the floor. I was in the second row, but Arya motioned for me to come forward. "This is Pat. She is one of our advanced students."

I walked slowly up, keeping my head lowered, while my heart thumped loudly. I looked down at Swami Rama's feet, unable to look up to where Swami Rama sat on an elevated dais. I knelt down and he touched me on the head, blessing me. I inhaled deeply, trying to calm myself. I was totally in awe of this enlightened being.

As a student of educational psychology, I was invited to participate in meetings with a group that included PhD psychologists, psychology students and medical doctors who met at the Meditation Center. My daily meditation seemed to improve my concentration. I read and absorbed my college texts very quickly. My mind seemed to focus like a sponge, and I easily got straight As in all my classes. I was excited and happy pursuing my dream of enlightenment that I'd had since ninth grade. I was also about to get involved in cutting-edged biofeedback research for my master's thesis.

My husband Bob did not like to practice yoga or meditate, but he did follow the rules of yama (do no harm). After completing a very lengthy application and getting references from many people, including my mother and friends in the military, Bob was granted conscientious objector status. He would serve his country, but he would not kill any living thing, or any other human. Things had been very scary, and he still faced possibly being sent to the front as a medic or sent away to a job in another state. We really didn't know what was going to happen. Before he was drafted the lottery started, and Bob ended up with a high number. He wasn't going to be drafted after all. He had a good job with the State of Minnesota, doing statistical research. He seemed supportive of my work, just not interested in yoga.

We drifted further apart. Bob stopped at the Triangle Bar on his way home from his research job In St. Paul. He said, "I need to relax after work. It's a thirty-minute drive into the sun on that bloody freeway. My eyes need a break."

The Triangle was pretty quiet and dark at 5:30 pm, about the time he arrived and joined the regulars. The musicians the bar was famous for like Dave Ray and Spider John Koener didn't arrive until 8, 9 or 10 pm depending on how they felt, and usually just on weekends, but they might just show up anytime. That was when things got crowded and noisy. If Bob wasn't home by 7 pm. I'd take dinner to him at the bar. The regulars were impressed by my homemade vegetarian pizza. After we ate dinner, I sat in a booth by myself drinking water while Bob played pool and drank beer at the bar. When the crowds arrived, other people joined me in my booth. I made line drawings of people as I sat repeating my mantra in my mind. I tried not to talk to anyone. If they wanted to talk, I motioned for them to write or draw in my sketch book.

Eventually Bob got tired, and we went home to our lower duplex apartment just across the freeway from The Triangle. I crawled into bed all alone, while Bob stayed up for one last beer.

CHAPTER 5

The Menninger Research Foundation 1971

IN THE SPRING OF 1971, Bob drove me to the Greyhound bus stop in Minneapolis. I was confident. It seemed like I was close to finding the answers to my deepest questions. Meditation controlled the guilt and insecurity I'd had since childhood. My 23rd birthday was just a few days away. I'd received a grant and an invitation to do some research on my thesis at the Menninger Research Foundation, which was centered in Topeka, Kansas at that time.

I pulled my thick long red hair behind my ears and held it there with a headband, I'd long since freed it from my childhood braids and center part. I adjusted my blouse to make sure I looked nice but didn't show too much cleavage. I'd never traveled on my own without my husband or my family. My suitcase was packed with books, notebooks, and pens and just enough clothes to get by for the week.

I sat in my bus seat with my back straight as I practiced my yoga meditation. My mind concentrated on my breath as I took deep inhalations into my stomach and then slowly let the air seep out my nose. I tried to concentrate on an imaginary vision of light. But instead of seeing the light, my mind wandered back over the story of how I'd gotten here.

In my mind I saw the letter I'd written that had opened this door.

Dear Dr. Green:

I'm a graduate student in educational psychology at the University of Minnesota and a student of Dr. Arya, one of Swami Rama's disciples. I want to write my thesis on using biofeedback with children who have learning and behavioral problems. I have read some of your work on biofeedback and I'm interested in researching how this might be possible. Could I come down and visit this spring?"

I just couldn't believe it. In response to that letter Dr Green invited me to come to the Menninger Research Center and see where Swami Rama had been tested and had proved he could control his autonomic nervous system. Dr Green was going to share his unpublished research papers with me.

I arrived on Monday, March 15, 1971, as per Dr. Green's request - ready to report to the lab on Tuesday. I brought some Indian dahl with me which I ate cold for dinner in my room. I enjoyed the total quiet of being in a room all by myself. I didn't need to cook dinner for Bob or anyone else. I didn't turn on the T.V. I just sat up straight with my legs crossed on my motel room bed and practiced meditation. I repeated my mantra again and again, clearing my mind of everything except the sound of my words reverberating in my mind.

I got up early Tuesday morning, March 16th, and took a taxi over to the lab where Dr. Green gave me a tour. "This is the room where we hooked Swami Rama up and we could observe him through this one-way glass."

I stared at the maze of electrodes, and the flat cold table the Swami must have lain on. *Did he sit up cross-legged there on the table?* I wondered but was too shy to say aloud.

Surprisingly Dr. Green asked me, "Would you like to try it?"

"Yes, definitely," I answered, without attempting to conceal my enthusiasm. I thought about sitting up cross-legged but, seeing as it was a bed, I lay down on it. It felt cool and hard, just like an examination table in a doctor's office. Dr. Green's assistant used a cold sticky paste to attach electrodes all over my head. I tried to get into a meditative state, all the while knowing I was being observed through the one-way mirror.

The EEG (electroencephalograph) machine in the next room recorded my brain waves on a continuous sheet of paper, with four lines - one for each brain wave: Delta waves, 0.5-3 Hz - deep sleep; Theta waves, 3.5-7.5, thought to be a creative meditative state; Alpha waves 8-12 Hz - a relaxed state; and Beta waves, 12-38 Hz, which normally dominate when people are awake and active.

I felt very exposed with my brainwaves being revealed to Dr. Green. In the darkened room I closed my eyes and practiced progressive relaxation. As I took deep slow breaths from my stomach, I relaxed each part of my body thinking, *My toes feel relaxed and heavy, My lower legs are heavy and relaxed,* while the machine in the next room recorded my brain waves. My mind wandered; I couldn't concentrate on my mantra. I thought just a minute had passed, but I'd been there 30 minutes when Dr. Green's assistant came in and disconnected me.

When I walked into the next room, I watched Dr. Green tear the print-out off the machine, staring at it for a long time. I wondered, *Did I do something wrong?* I peeked over his shoulder trying to figure it out. Finally, I asked, "What does it say?"

"Well, you generated an unusual amount of Theta waves," Dr. Green said.

I gasped silently; that was exactly what Dr. Green was training people to do through biofeedback. Although I tried to get into a deep meditative state; it had seemed like I was only being my normal spacey self. That's how I felt when I just let my mind wander, relaxed. It was as if the Theta waves showed how I felt when I looked out the window while washing dishes; my hands submerged in warm water, not what

I felt when I was trying to meditate. Maybe I was trying too hard to meditate.

Dr Green allowed me to go into his research files and do research for my thesis. He kept an extensive collection of papers taken from different periodicals of the time. This was a gold mine, since in 1971 there was very little research on biofeedback. Biofeedback was the use of temperature meters or brain wave monitors to teach people how to control their autonomic nervous system, such as redirecting blood flow to the hands to stop a migraine headache or putting your mind into a relaxed state to counteract anxiety.

The next night the Greens invited me to have dinner with them. Their home was a modest bungalow very close to the research center. Dr. Elmer Green and his wife Dr. Alicia Green worked together to create a marvelous vegetarian meal that featured almonds, brown rice, and vegetables. I felt so blessed because it was my 23rd birthday. I didn't tell them. That evening Pat, Elmer Green's adult daughter asked, "Would you like to go hear Swami Rama? He's going to be speaking at Unity Village tomorrow night."

"Yes, I'd love to go. I met Swami Rama at Dr. Arya's house in Minnesota last year. I'd really like to see him again. But I don't have a car. I took a bus down here for my research."

"You can ride with us," Alicia Green offered.

"Thanks so much," I answered calmly, but my legs felt like jumping up and down in my bellbottoms. The next evening, we drove for 45 minutes past flat cornfields to Unity Village in Jackson County, Missouri. I brought my suitcase along because Alicia was going to drop me off in Topeka after the lecture to catch the bus back to Minneapolis. We parked and walked into a large hall packed with people. The crowd buzzed in anticipation of a lecture by a real Indian Swami. A hush fell over the room as Swami Rama walked on stage wearing a beautiful white shawl thrown over his shoulders. He spoke flawless English with a lovely Indian accent. His voice rose and fell with a mesmerizing rhythm.

"Let me explain yoga," he broke the silence. "Yoga is not a religion; it is a yoke, a discipline. Prana, the breath, is the key. It is the key to self-realization. Self-realization is the aim of life. Both the East and the West agree on this goal. The first step in life is to know thyself. Listen to your own heart and follow its guidance...."

I didn't really listen to what was being said. I concentrated on my own prana. I let his words absorb into me as I felt air slowly entering my body. As I released my breath, I concentrated on sending peace throughout the room. The vibrations reverberated through my whole being. This was my path. This was the guru Vivekananda said would appear when I was ready.

After his talk, Dr. Green's daughter and I hurried up front. *Would he remember me from when we met in Dr. Arya's attic?*

I held out my hand, but before I could say anything Swami Rama looked at me with his piercing eyes. I felt like he was reading my mind. "I remember you," he said. "You're one of Arya's students. We met in the attic. Did he tell you that I foresaw you being a great yoga teacher?"

"No, I didn't know," I replied, taking a deep breath, practicing prana to stay calm while my heart thumped in my chest. *Yes, this is my guru.* I pictured the moment I'd first met him in Dr. Arya's attic, my legs crossed and my back totally straight sitting on the floor with the other yoga students. Swami Rama had picked me out of the crowd to come up. He'd blessed me by touching my head.

"Can you stay here tonight? I want to give you some special instructions," Swami Rama said.

"I don't know. I don't have a reservation. I have to take a bus back to Minneapolis tonight," I said.

"Oh, I'm sure Unity Village will have an empty cabin. I'll see if I can get one for you." said Swami Rama. "You can catch the bus tomorrow."

I was sure Unity Village wouldn't have room for me, and besides, I didn't have money for one. But I was wrong. They found me a place in cabin twenty-four. I'm not sure who paid for it. I used a phone at the center to make a collect call to Bob, to tell him I'd be staying an extra evening. He was fine with the change.

Swami Rama told me where his cabin was and asked me to come after dark, so no one would think something strange was going on. This was a great honor. I was going to receive special instructions that would hasten my journey to enlightenment.

As soon as I got my one small suitcase placed in my room, it was dark, and I made my way to cabin number eight.

The guest cabins at Unity Village in 1971 were very modest - just one room with a bed and a bath. I walked down the path quietly. No one saw me knock at the door of cabin number eight.

"Come in," Swami Rama said. His eyes gleamed as a huge smile spread across his broad face, "I'm so glad that you have finally come."

"Am I late?" I asked, embarrassed.

"No, you're not late, but I've been waiting for you for such a long time," he answered. "We were meant to meet in this life."

What is he talking about? I wondered to myself.

"You will become a famous yoga teacher and have many dedicated students. You can come to India and work with me."

"I don't want to be famous; I just want to be enlightened," I answered, expressing my profound wish, and deepest desire.

"Of course, you will be enlightened, but first we must be together," he said sitting down on the bed and indicating that I should sit next to him.

Since he was a monk, I decided this should be okay, but when he kissed me. I pushed him away, totally confused.

My mind balked: *stop now.* This was not anything Arya had talked about. But Arya also said Swami wasn't just a man, he was enlightened; he knew everything. He knew my future and my past.

"What do you mean by this?" I asked licking his kiss off my lips. "I thought you were celibate?"

"No, I've never taken any vows."

I got up ready to leave, my knees shaking.

"Please stay, I've been waiting for you forever. You are my wife from a previous life. It is a miracle that we have met now. I've not been with any woman in this life," His deep black eyes implored me with a sense of urgency.

"But... but... I'm married now, in this life," I said.

Earlier I'd believed in free love, but Arya had taught me that a man and a woman fused their auras, their sacred selves and to switch partners was to confuse one's very essence. I didn't want to hurt my husband or confuse myself.

"Oh, but we must. That's why we've come together on this sacred night," Swami Rama said.

This was an incredible happening. I must have been in India in a previous life. His presence made me feel I was remembering that past life. I could feel myself floating around in his house wearing a sari being a dutiful wife.

He took out a necklace with a Star of David and placed it around my neck, whispering, "This is to remind you of our past life together," into my ear.

What he was saying must be true. He was my teacher's guru; therefore, he was my guru too. Arya had told us again and again how his guru Swami Rama could do no wrong.

If he was my husband, and he couldn't do any wrong, this must be right. It must be what is meant to be. I acquiesced. I'd never had strong boundaries, I'd never learned to defend myself, *against an all-knowing guru. Who was I?*

Swami Rama spent the night trying to prove that he'd been my husband more than once; by climaxing numerous times, and he made sure I did too. I'd just fallen asleep, and he'd be at it again. I was truly convinced that I had been his wife in a previous life. He paced the room, full of nervous energy, I felt a wifely desire to calm him, to protect him.

The next morning a nervous pushy guy, like one might see hawking things at a carnival stopped by the cabin. Swami Rama introduced him as his business manager. They discussed the crowd and the take of the night before. "That was a really good crowd wasn't it, one of the best you've had. You're becoming quite the draw." The guy carried on, about how to get crowds. It didn't seem like a very spiritual discussion to me, but maybe Swami Rama needed his help to reach people in the material world.

While this guy was talking, Swami Rama chain-smoked cigarettes.

Next there was an interview with a young lady from the newspaper. He introduced me, "This is my disciple, Pat, from the University of Minnesota," he said, smiling at me.

The interviewer looked at me, her eyes wide with excitement.

I greeted her, but I felt embarrassed that she thought I was already close to enlightenment. I felt wifey, but not enlightened.

The reporter interviewed him, taking detailed notes of his achievements at the Menninger Research Center, and his past accomplishments in India.

I felt uncomfortable with this self-promotion, but this was the way of the western world. If he was to get his message out, he'd have to do these things.

I caught the bus and returned to Minneapolis, to continue my studies and my wifely duties with my husband of this life. When I walked in the door back home everything was quiet. Bob, my tall, handsome, blond, blue-eyed, husband was at the bar again. I didn't care because I was still walking on air. I fingered the necklace around my neck, assuring myself that it had not been a dream.

Shortly after I returned from my trip to Menninger and Unity Village, I wrote a long thank you note to the Greens. Initially I was in a very good place, I wrote, "A lot of things have happened since I returned. The trip itself seems to have done a lot of good... Every day my eyes open a little more and the world becomes a strange succession of walking through thoughts. Time ceases to exist yet constantly turns."

As I reflected on my amazing experience with my husband of a previous life, my mind churned in a different direction. *Maybe Swami Rama was right. He was my real husband. All Bob wanted to do was hang out at the bar and drink.*

Now I'd seen Swami Rama as a man, but I kept thinking: *if I was Swami Rama's wife, then we should tell all and become man and wife again.* I called him, again and again, until finally I reached him.

"No, no, we can't do that. I have an ashram, I have disciples, we can't do that now," he said.

My head was shaking, as I lowered the phone back down into its cradle. I couldn't accept this rejection. *Surely, he is mistaken. Things are different now; this is America; people would understand. Love conquers all.*

CHAPTER 6

Superwoman
1971-1972

A FEW WEEKS AFTER my phone conversation with Swami Rama, he came on a visit to Minneapolis. I was very excited when Arya told me that Swami had requested a private audience with me. *Maybe he'd reconsidered. Maybe we could be together in this life.* My marriage was hopeless, Bob was constantly at the bar. He went to work, I went to work, I came home and cooked dinner. We hardly talked anymore.

Arya was proud that Swami Rama had singled out one of his students for special attention. He totally believed in the guru-disciple tradition. He had accepted Swami Rama as his guru, and he would follow him for the rest of his life. Arya instructed me "You need to go to the Leamington Hotel at exactly 10:00 am."

The Leamington was an old hotel downtown built in 1912, and still advertised itself as *the Upper Midwest's largest finest and most complete hotel*. President Eisenhower had even stayed there. I'd never been there, so I dressed to meet my new love. I put on a long dress that showed every curve. I wore my long, red hair flowing almost to my waist. I didn't have any really nice shoes, so I went barefoot as I often did. When I looked down at my feet, the flowing skirt covered them up just fine. Before I got in the car, I picked a bouquet of apple blossoms for him from my backyard. A heavenly smell arose from the seat as the petals fell everywhere.

At the allotted time, I parked my car in the parking lot and walked to the hotel, the large square building towered over me. My heart thumped loudly while I quietly slipped through the lobby, my bare feet peeping out as my long skirt swished. I stepped into the elevator and pushed the button for the 10th floor. I hoped nobody else would get into the elevator, but it stopped on the second floor. A gentleman got on in a three-piece suit. His eyes unnerved me. Those eyes stared at my dress and my bare feet. I smiled at him as I got out My bouquet trailed apple blossoms petals as I made my way to Swami Rama's door.

I knocked on the door and Swami Rama opened it, and with a broad smile said, "My, you look lovely."

He took the apple blossoms and set them aside. He turned me around and unzipped my dress without another word. I watched as it fell on the floor next to the bed. I wanted to ask about our conversation and if he'd changed his mind, but he just spun me around again and pushed me back down onto the bed. I felt like a rag doll as he thrust into me, not giving me any time to respond. After he emptied himself into me; he got up and left the room. I felt like the energy had been sucked out of my soul. I closed my eyes, wanting just to sleep. Then I heard water running. *Oh, he's just having a shower. He'll be back, and we'll talk about my divorce, and our getting together in this life,* I thought.

Instead, he came out of the shower and walked over to the bed holding a wad of toilet paper.

"Here, wipe yourself quickly. The doctors are meeting with me in 20 minutes."

"What?" my eyes snapped open. *Shit, I'm not dressed to meet them.* I thought. I'd met them at the psychologist's group at Arya's house. I quickly put on my dress and raced to the elevators, worried that I might run into them. I made it to my car and drove home. At home I lay down on my bed. I felt like my life's energy had been sucked out. I just wanted to cry; there was no hope. I would never do that again. That was not what I wanted in this life. I wanted to be enlightened, not fucked. Finally, wasted from crying, I fell asleep.

The next time I went to the Meditation Center, Arya called me into his private office. I sat down on the floor cross-legged and looked up at him dressed in his white robes. "I received a complaint from the Leamington Hotel, concerning the day you were there. The Meditation Center rented the room for him, and our reputation is on the line. They said that Swami Rama had a prostitute visit his room. They are an upstanding business hotel and don't want to rent to people who have loose women visit their rooms during the day. Could that have been you?"

"No, I certainly don't think so. I'm sure that wasn't me," I lied. I let myself believe the lie just as I learned to do as a child when Mother confronted me.

Arya looked down at me, perhaps wanting to believe me, but doubting my words. To him, evil American women were trying to seduce his celibate enlightened guru who was beyond the material plane.

I sat totally still, repeating my mantra, but the meaning of the words transformed themselves in my mind, *I'm not a whore, I'm not a whore, I'm a graduate student, a teacher, a disciple, and most of all his guru's dutiful wife from a past life*. And now, now I just wanted to be enlightened. Arya just didn't know the truth.

"Ok, I believe you," Arya said.

I left, relieved that I had not betrayed Swami Rama nor Arya. I still believed that I was his wife from a previous life. In this life I determined never to be placed in a situation like that again. My mind raced, what did I really want? I wanted out of this rat race, maybe I just needed to become a celibate myself, and dedicate my life totally to yoga. I fingered the Star of David necklace Swami Rama had given me that fateful night. I didn't want to be his wife, but I still wanted enlightenment.

A few weeks later the phone rang. It was Arya. I wanted to tell him about my new resolve, but before I could open my mouth he said, "I just spoke with Swami Rama. He asked me to call you and explain your duty in this life is to remain with your husband."

"Oh, but I'd really like to dedicate my life to the study of yoga," I said, just trying to articulate my thoughts.

Arya cut me off saying, "If you get divorced, you will not be welcome at the Meditation Center."

I took a deep breath. I really wanted to slam the receiver down, but instead I said, "Okay," in a very soft voice as I swallowed hard, trying to hold back my tears.

I took it as my fate in this life to take care of my husband. Bob and I moved to Lindstrom, Minnesota, a small town. We wanted to be closer to nature away from the drugs and the bars. I took part in fewer and fewer activities at the Meditation Center. We rented a small unheated cabin so we could save money to buy a house. Bob started to drink more and more. One day I came home from my job teaching at the juvenile detention center, and Bob was off in the city with his friends. I fell asleep. At 2 a.m. a loud knock woke me up. I put on my robe and opened the door. We didn't have a phone.

"Hello ma'am," said a police officer.

I blinked my eyes in shock. *Had Bob been killed? What was wrong?*

"We have your husband at the police station. He was driving under the influence."

"What?" I asked, shaking my head.

"Is Robert Stierna your husband?"

"Yes."

"We have him at the police station. His bail is $600. If you have it, you can come pick him up."

The police looked around at the unheated cabin wrinkling their noses. They let the door slam as they left.

I slumped back into bed, devastated. *How could he do this?* I had $600 in the bank. It was saved towards a down-payment on a house.

The next day I stopped by at the bank and pulled six $100 bills out of our account. It was all the money I'd saved during the last four months. Then I drove to the town jail to bail him out. When I walked in, a policeman was lounging with his feet up on the desk.

"I'm here to pick up Robert Stierna," I said.

"Do you have $600?" he asked, looking surprised.

"Yes, I do," as I took the six $100 bills out of my wallet. He jumped up and went to get a large ring of keys. I felt like I was in some old western movie, only this time it was for real.

Bob crawled into the car; his dirty stringy hair plastered to his head. He turned towards me with bloodshot eyes, "I'm sorry," he said, quickly turning to look down at the floor.

My clenched jaw relaxed, but my brain still buzzed with anger. "I had to pull the money I'd been saving for a down-payment to pay your bail."

"I know, I'm sorry, it won't happen again," he repeated, still staring at the floor. Later I learned that stopping drinking had been impossible for his father, and his grandfather before that.

My anger melted. I knew he didn't mean to mess up. When Bob went to court, his license was revoked for six months. I drove him everywhere, besides going to my job, and cooking all the meals in the unheated cabin. All I needed was a cape and a tight-fitting swimsuit and I'd be Superwoman. It was a hopeless task, but I persevered. I believed what Swami Rama said: this was my task, my duty in this life.

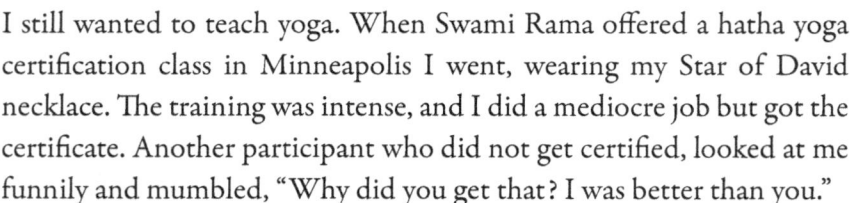

I still wanted to teach yoga. When Swami Rama offered a hatha yoga certification class in Minneapolis I went, wearing my Star of David necklace. The training was intense, and I did a mediocre job but got the certificate. Another participant who did not get certified, looked at me funnily and mumbled, "Why did you get that? I was better than you."

I just shook my head, and said, "I don't know," and felt ashamed. Maybe I didn't deserve it. I took the certificate, but every time I looked at it, I felt ashamed. The girl was right, she was better than I was.

After the class, I walked up to Swami Rama and asked, "What can I do about my husband's drinking?"

He answered, "He's your child. You need to take care of him. He needs you."

I felt a like a dead albatross had been placed around my neck. Yet I continued to wear Swami Rama's necklace and persevere in my study of yoga.

In August of 1971, the growing Meditation Center had a retreat along the St. Croix River. I was excited to go and as the family driver I took Bob along, even though he wasn't excited about yoga. We threw our tent and clothes into the car and set out. All the food was going to be cooked by the yoga group. I wrote a special cookbook for the group as being a vegetarian, I had more experience, than most people. It was going to be seven days of living like at an ashram in India, with daily meditation and ritual. After driving 45 minutes from our cabin in Lindstrom, we set up our tent in its designated spot just a short walk from the St. Croix River.

As a teacher who worked with emotionally disturbed children, I was included with the psychologists. People moved quietly and peacefully through the woods. We meditated, chanted and sang. We bathed in the river. One couple even got married in a Hindu ceremony by the campfire.

Arya passed out a new handout on having a mantra. I read it over. There were bullet points listed about the relationship between the initiate and the initiator. Arya had been my initiator and I still respected him. I continued to practice my meditation daily and I was training to be an initiator myself. My eyes focused on the moral and spiritual guidelines. I had no problem at all with non-violence, and I'd been a vegetarian since I was 18 years old. I focused on number 2 "Loyalty to one sexual partner, taking your sexual relationships and marriage with the seriousness they deserve." *How ironic,* I thought, *Arya takes this seriously, I wish Swami Rama had done so too, wife from a previous life or not.* Something did not seem right, but I wanted to learn yoga. I wanted to be part of this group, so I continued to attend lectures at the Meditation Center and practice daily meditation.

That fall, before the weather turned cold, Bob got his license back, and we found a house to buy. We borrowed the down-payment money from my teachers' credit union. I didn't pay much attention to anything but the yard and the lake just across the street. The whole neighborhood, called Coon Lake Beach was filled with 100-foot pine trees. The trees calmed the wind and filled my soul with joy.

Bob was happy because he could walk home from the local drinking establishment, a bar called the Ramblers. This local watering hole was a dark, dismal place that smelled of dust and stale beer. Its dark interior consisted of a long counter for drinking at, a pool table and a few tables. I couldn't understand why even on bright sunny days, there were cars in the parking lot. Bob loved stopping there on his way home. He didn't have to worry about getting another ticket for driving under the influence. We got a dog. I lived at home with the dog and Bob lived at the bar.

I wanted to do my research project for my thesis using biofeedback at my work. I worked at a Juvenile Detention Center, and they gave permission for me to do biofeedback with my students. Yet I was unable to write the proposal. Every time I sat down to work on it, my mind went blank. After what had happened with Swami Rama, I just lost my confidence and didn't trust anything. I still wanted to study yoga, but I couldn't continue my research. I put the project on hold. After all, I had seven years to get it done.

The Meditation Center continued to grow and purchased 200 acres up north for the next retreat. That retreat was held June 25-July 2, 1972. Two hundred people, including families with children, attended. This time Swami Rama was there.

Dedicated followers of Arya and Swami Rama started working there in April, leaving their jobs, or coming on weekends without pay. The ground was still frozen when they cut the trails, made clearings, built latrines, put up structures. They built geodesic domes under the direction of a university professor and architect. I was honored to be included in the list of advisors to such a hardworking, selfless, and dedicated group of people. I wished I could be more involved, and I was happy when Bob said he couldn't go to the retreat.

Bob didn't want to take the time off from work or his visits to the Ramblers. I left the school as soon as I could after work. Working at the Juvenile Detention Center, I did not get summer vacations.

The Retreat Center was not yet finished. It was like visiting an undeveloped country. There were latrines, not flush toilets, and no running water, because the well had not been dug yet. The clouds rained mosquitos, and the long grass hid wood ticks. There was no TV or even electricity. The retreat was a reconstruction of an ashram in India. Every moment was structured to help us develop our spiritual awareness.

The morning started at 6:00 a.m. with hatha yoga exercise, 150 people did sun salutations in an open field led by an experienced teacher. While we waited for Swami Rama Arya explained how we should stand with our heads bowed when he appeared. This was not to worship him, but to honor his achievement of a higher state of consciousness. Swami came in bringing a harmonium and everyone stood in awe, until he motioned for us to sit. He played the harmonium and led us in chanting before starting our silent meditation. After meditation, we attended lectures.

I fell into the daily routine with gusto, wanting to belong and help out in the community, and attending every lecture.

The guys whispered about a secret meeting they'd attended with Swami Rama. They said, "He came to us with a rope dangling in front of his body which he said was attached to his penis. He tied this to a pail of water which he proceeded to lift using the rope and using his hips to swing from side to side. He let it down and untied it saying he could only do this because he was celibate."

How very strange, especially since I knew he wasn't celibate. I mulled this over in my mind, wondering *Why did he tell them this? Surely, I was his only wife from a previous life living at this time.*

I did not do any consulting and I kept my distance from the Swami. I wasn't interested in any more wifey experiences. Talking with fellow members of the Meditation Center, I found out that despite all the hard work, the Swami was not impressed by our retreat center, especially since a rat had eaten his favorite shawl.

CHAPTER 7

Going to India
1972-1973

MY EYES FILLED WITH COLOR from the delicate flowers that gently hung from the stem of the fuchsia plant as I placed it on the windowsill of my dull classroom at the Minnesota State Juvenile Detention Center. Their soft pink-purpleness brightened the room. This was my first teaching job and I'd been struggling to stay calm and keep the attention of a classroom of students who were released from their detention cabins to come to school on the prison grounds. At the university I was taught to use positive reinforcement and never to raise my voice with students. I reinforced good behavior and ignored bad behavior, always staying calm. I worked hard to make my classroom a positive place for these poor kids who were locked up away from their families.

It was the first class of the day. At first nobody seemed to notice the plant, but then a tall skinny boy noticed it. He got up and walked over it. He grabbed the delicate flowers and broke the stem crushing the flowers between his fingers.

I'd had enough. I yelled, "Don't do that, why would you do that?" My voice echoed throughout the room.

The whole class stopped and stared at me. One boy said, "We thought you didn't care."

I took stock and realized that these kids wanted me to show I cared, to show emotions, and not always be positive. After that we got on well, and I enjoyed creating lessons they were interested in. We made a newspaper and published it for the entire detention center. They made paper-mâché puppets and did a puppet show. I taught them progressive relaxation; they loved the feeling of getting "high" without drugs. I enjoyed going to work, but I still wasn't motivated to do my thesis; furthermore, I really wanted summer vacations, which the Juvenile Detention Center didn't have.

My spiritual progress was still my number one goal. A group from the Meditation Center was planning a trip to India and I wanted to go too. I'd saved money from my job, and I even found a job at a public school that would start after I returned from India. Although Bob had a drinking problem, he'd always been there for me. I cautiously approached him. I also knew that in the Indian tradition I would need his permission to go on this trip.

"A group from the Meditation Center in Minneapolis is planning to go to Swami Rama's ashram in India in February and I'd like to go with them. I've saved the money. My new job will start when I get back. I really want to go. I'll just be gone a month."

Bob stared at me and shook his head. "That's a long time."

"I'll write to you. Maybe we could do an experiment in telepathic communication," I suggested, holding my breath, taking a long shot. We'd only read about telepathy but had never done any. I hoped this would help him feel all right with this. We hadn't been separated for more than a week since we'd gotten married in 1967, six years earlier.

Bob looked at me with sad puppy eyes. "Okay", he sighed. He loved me and respected me. He never stood in the way of something I really wanted. We set March 8, 1973, at 10:00 a.m. New Delhi time as the time that we would communicate via telepathy. Internet did not exist yet and international phone calls were expensive and unreliable.

I got a passport, a new 35mm camera, 12 rolls of film, and a Panasonic cassette tape recorder. I wanted to have pictures and sounds from my first flight in a jet plane. Before I finalized the trip, I sat down and wrote a rough draft of a short letter to Swami Rama.

> *Dear Swami Rama,*
> *I want to come on the trip to the ashram in India with the group from the meditation center in February. I'm coming to study yoga, and I want to be sure that we will not be getting together for anything intimate again.*
> *Sincerely, your disciple,*
> *Pat*

I carefully typed the final version and mailed it to Swami Rama. I shoved my rough draft into the back of my desk. Swami Rama called me on the phone and said, "Of course you can come with the Meditation Center. You don't have anything to worry about.".

The morning of my departure Bob drove me to the airport and my mother came too. Mother seemed very nervous, as if she was worried that I'd never return. I didn't pay attention, except for the churning of my stomach in excitement. This was a dream come true, I was actually going to India, where people had practiced yoga for centuries, where they respected all life, and did not eat meat. Bob and Mom got to wait with me at the terminal, and we hugged goodbye just before I boarded the plane with other members from the Meditation Center

We flew first to New York and then boarded our Pan American east-bound flight 002 "Around the World Flight." Our 747 jumbo jet had just started flying three years ago in 1970. We were scheduled to stop in London, Frankfurt, Istanbul, Beirut, and Tehran before we would finally arrive in New Delhi, India. I wondered what it would be like to go all the way around the world instead of just halfway. First stop was Heathrow in London, and I gleefully ran on and off the plane, skipping through the airport for just one hour. Then I was back on the same huge 747 and up in the air again. Looking down as we started to descend, I saw carefully arranged squares of land, exactly the neat organization I would expect in Germany. We ran off the plane and Phil, a fellow yoga student, purchased another camera in addition to the large movie camera he was carrying. I got some Belgian chocolate. Then when I went to board the plane, I was pulled into a private room by a very strong look-ing German lady. She patted me all over, patting my hair piled on my head. I was shocked. There hadn't been any security at any of the other airports, but in Germany Palestinian terrorists had attacked the Israeli Olympic team in 1972. They were still on high alert for terrorists one year later. I felt this was ridiculous. I certainly wasn't a terrorist.

Up in the air again, I looked out the window and saw the French Alps covered in snow. Our next stop was Istanbul, Turkey. The sun had set, and it was dark. We got off and wandered around an almost empty airport. There were a few bearded men hawking exotic rugs and hoo-kahs. Everything was a reddish golden color in the dim lights of the airport. The men stared at me and my skin crawled, so I hurried to get back on the plane.

The next stop was Beirut, Lebanon. It was 2 a.m. and no one was around. As I stepped off the plane, I was in awe of the lights from a beautiful city that sparkled on the hill to my left. The airport, though deserted, was immaculate, with beautiful chandeliers hanging above the counters. My heart would grieve for this place destroyed in the 1975 war, just a couple of years later.

From there we went to Tehran in Iran. It was morning now. I was still awake ready to experience another airport, another world, when the loudspeaker announced, "All passengers remain onboard while the plane refuels."

My heart sank as I heard these words. "Why can't we get off?" No one really knew why, but they all had theories. "They think it's too dangerous," was one rumor. Danger, what danger? I wondered, as I stayed on the plane.

We took off again and we flew over the desert. The sun was blaring down, reflecting off endless white sands. There, climbing up a hill of sand, I saw a real line of camels. As we ascended into the clouds I thought, *Our next stop will be India.*

The seatbelt light came on. *This is it. We will be landing soon.* Instead, the stewardess said, "The bar is open, free drinks for everyone."

My eyes opened wide in disgust; free drinks were the last thing we needed. The passenger behind me was not part of our group, and he was already drunk. His alcoholic breath rose into the air every time he opened his mouth.

The stewardess continued, "We're landing in Islamabad, Pakistan, to drop off an engine and pick up some stranded passengers."

This was the first time we'd heard of this. More adventure, now I'd get to see Pakistan too. This time they let us get off the plane. I jumped into the aisle as soon as possible to beat the drunk off the plane and join the other passengers from my group. The sun blasted down as we were motioned into a building. Inside was hotter than outside. The air-conditioning didn't work. Outside at least there was a hot breeze. The concrete on the flat runways shimmered in the sun. The airport was surrounded by miles of barbed wire not fastened to fence posts, but in rolls over ten feet high. Phil lifted his camera to take a picture. A guard lifted his rifle and shook his head. Phil quickly lowered his camera.

"Yikes, what was that about?" I asked

"The India-Pakistan war just ended in 1971, but they still aren't friends. The airport is a military installation, and we are on our way to India. We could be spies," Phil said.

I shivered as I stared at the barbed wire with no way out. Finally, after three hours, they called us back on the plane. It took off full of stranded passengers and carrying an extra engine that needed repair. It bounced down when it finally landed in New Delhi. They rolled out stairs and we carried our luggage down the staircase to the tarmac.

When I finally got to my hotel, it was still morning, but I was beyond exhausted. I'd been awake for over 20 hours either on a plane or exploring airport terminals. I could barely walk. I was glad I wasn't staying on for the whole way around the world; I was ready to crash. There was a knock on the door. "Come, get to the bus, we are going on a tour of New Delhi." I dutifully crawled out of bed and boarded the bus tour. At this point we were joined by followers of Swami Rama from all over the USA. People came from Chicago, Milwaukee, Pennsylvania, and California, in addition to our group from Minneapolis.

I wasn't at all interested in a tour. My eyes kept closing and my stomach churned as unreal scenes flew by the bus: a camel carried sticks; workers built buildings with bamboo scaffoldings; a ragged little boy rode by, sitting on a pile of dung in a cart pulled by a horse; an old man gathered cardboard up from the road, looking as if he planned to make a dwelling out of it. In those days you never saw homeless people on the streets in America. Then they dumped us out of the bus to walk around an ancient pillar. I shuffled my way around, following our group. When we got back on the bus, ready to go back to sleep, a plump gentleman who happened to be a minister, stood up and asked, "Has anyone lost a bill of any denomination?"

Surely, he's not talking about me. I woke up enough to check the secret pocket I'd sewn into my bra for an emergency. The $100 bill I'd put there was gone.

I walked up and whispered, "I lost a hundred-dollar bill that was hidden in my clothes." I was embarrassed and didn't tell him where it had been hidden. In 1973, $100 was a lot of money. In India at that time the dollar value was seven to one. I took the bill and put it in my purse, not my bra.

Finally, they took us back to the hotel, where I thankfully got to sleep. I woke up the next morning early and wandered out on the street in front of the hotel, taking a few pictures and shocked by the poverty I saw all around. Just across the street from the hotel, a potter worked, his wares out in front of the shack where it looked like he lived. There were people everywhere.

The next day we all climbed aboard the rickety bus for our trip to Rishikesh, NE of New Delhi, the location of Swami Rama's ashram. The driver tied our luggage onto the roof of the bus. I was sure it would fall off. I carried my 35 mm camera and a tape recorder with me, in addition to my purse, not allowing them out of my touch. We travelled all day, the roads getting smaller and smaller. It was totally dark when we arrived at the ashram.

In total darkness I stumbled up the narrow concrete stairs to the women's dorm room and collapsed on a four-inch mattress laid upon a cot-like structure. I breathed in warm moist tropical air, grateful to be on a still flat surface instead of a plane or bouncing bus.

My brain entered into deep sleep until sunlight tickled my eyelids in the morning. Peeking out, I saw an unfamiliar ceiling. *Where am I?* My mind questioned the strange smell of jasmine floating in the warm air. *I've arrived, I'm at the ashram in Rishikesh.*

I jumped out of bed and took in the long narrow room with three cot-like beds and a door at the back of the room. A row of windowed doors beckoned me towards the light. In three steps I was out that door standing on a patio that overlooked a sea of eager students sitting cross-legged in the garden below me. My eyes wandered out beyond to the holy Ganges River and then further east the foothills of the Himalayan mountains rose up into the sky. My mouth dropped open in awe of my being present in such a place.

As I stood there staring at the view, a small dark-haired woman came up and said, "Hello, my name's Megan, I'm your roommate, I've got the cot next to you."

"Hi, I'm Pat," I answered. We hit it off right then. It felt like I'd finally met my sister. I'd grown up with brothers, and always longed for a sister. I learned she played violin in an orchestra and shared that I'd played flute in a youth orchestra. She had gorgeous shoulder-length black hair and a sincere sad smile.

Megan and I turned towards a very young girl just rubbing the sleep out of her eyes. She introduced herself with her Indian name "Kimaya" She was just nineteen years old, from southwestern Minnesota. She had kinky shoulder-length blonde hair and innocent eyes. Her enthusiasm for life was infectious.

Life here was like the retreats we'd had in Minnesota. We woke up at 6:00 a.m. We dressed quickly to join the hatha yoga exercises out in the garden. They were led by Linda, but now she had taken her vows to be a monk, she wore a yellow robe and was called Ma Yogalina. She seemed like a very advanced soul. She was very quiet and never spoke except to instruct us in our yoga poses.

Wonderful vegetarian meals were made by our Indian cook. We learned to eat Indian style using our right hand to pick up the food with our chapati, a round flat Indian bread.

Once a day an untouchable came to clean our toilets and take out the trash. She was very thin and wore a sweater with a hole in it. We were instructed not to talk to her or give her anything. I disobeyed, and smiled at her, and gave her a small Japanese paper fan. She was overjoyed and smiled and bowed.

Amara, a very nice upper class Indian woman who was helping out at the Ashram explained to us, "A woman who walks alone without a man is considered to be a prostitute. It is so disgusting to see these American hippie women who come here and travel around all by themselves."

I was shocked and disappointed by these negative comments. I thought these hippie women just don't understand Indian culture. *Maybe they shouldn't be running around like that in this country, but I'm sure they're not prostitutes.*

Another day we went to visit a Hindu temple in Rishikesh. Just the women went, accompanied by a male driver to ensure their reputations. I was glad I didn't have to live like that at home. When we arrived, I marveled at the bright colors that adorned the walls of the temple. An old man, advanced in hatha yoga, showed us how flexible he was despite his old age - he could even put his legs behind his neck. They gave us a book with pictures of him in amazing poses. The temple punjari (priest) took us into a private room separate from our driver. He looked at us intently and asked, "What yoga is Swami Rama teaching you in America.?"

"He teaches us meditation, and we do hatha yoga too," we answered, surprised by his question. He nodded his head and said, "Hmm."

On the way home, we couldn't help but share our feeling, that the Punjari did not seem to like Swami Rama.

We were to stay here for almost an entire month. After the first week Megan and I missed western music. Megan had left her violin at home. Along with the tape recorder I had brought along a classical Bach tape. After lunch one day, Megan and I were relaxing listening to the tape when she confided in me.

Megan said, "You know what Swami Rama told me? He told me I was his wife in a previous life."

My gut wrenched, and I felt like I'd fallen into the pit, just as when Masayoshi betrayed me. But I calmly said, "That's interesting. He told me the same thing."

Megan's eyes got wide as she stared back at me. As I kept my outward calm my heart raced with anger. Swami Rama the great guru had lied. We didn't say anything more about it, remembering of course that we weren't supposed to have said anything at all.

That evening I removed the necklace with the Star of David from my neck and threw it into the bottom of my suitcase.

My mind that had been closed in a dream of absolute fidelity, finally opened. I started to watch what was going on around me. Kimaya kept going down to see Swami Rama in individual sessions. She came back very excited. I asked her, "What is Swami Rama doing with you?"

"Oh, he is raising my kundalini," she said, her eyes glowing out of control. The kundalini is the latent female energy believed to be coiled at the base of the spine.

"How is he doing that?", I asked, more doubts rising into my consciousness.

"Well, he put his hand at the base of my spine to straighten my back, and then he kissed me."

I put two and two together and got six. I thought to myself: *He is seducing this young girl, and she doesn't even know it. I'm not the only wife, and now he's working on this young girl.* I felt I needed to do something about this, but what on earth could I do, just one stupid woman, in his ashram in India?

CHAPTER 8

The Confrontation in India
1973

THAT NIGHT I WENT to bed and closed my eyes. Multiple scenarios ran through my head. Whatever I did, it could be dangerous. I was in a foreign country. Swami Rama could decide to have me murdered for betrayal. I could get thrown out into the street. I'd paid for my room and board, yet I was his guest. This was his ashram. All alone in the world, lost in a foreign country, I tossed and turned. My body longed for security, any security. Maybe Bob was a drunk, but he never lied to me. He was my rock, he would protect me, if he was here. Thinking of my husband, I fell into a fitful sleep.

I awoke just before dawn feeling feverish, but I knew I didn't have a fever. My neck was stiff, my jaw felt like my teeth had been grinding together all night. There was a tightness in my chest as I remembered the revelations the night before. I slid out from under my covers and quietly snuck out on the balcony in my nightdress.

Sitting in a yoga pose with my back straight and my legs crossed, I prayed. I'd never really prayed before. The one prayer I'd tried to do as a child when I asked God to reveal the true religion to me had gone unanswered. All this time I'd been trying to find this truth through the study of yoga. Now the yoga guru had lied. I'd believed that finding a guru and following him would answer my burning questions. Now I wasn't looking for answers; I needed help, it was out of desperation that I prayed. Using yoga techniques, I calmed my racing heart, relaxed my neck muscles, unclenched my jaw. I didn't meditate. I didn't repeat my mantra over and over while concentrating on my breath. No, I asked God for guidance.

"Dear God, what should I do? What can I do to stop this abuse that I see before me?"

My heart reached out; my mind was empty, waiting for answers. My breath slowed and I stared into the horizon. In the foothills of the Himalayan mountains, I saw an image of light. The image grew and shimmered. It took on the shape of a human face, like the glowing face I'd seen in pictures of Jesus. Rays of light flowed out from its center and penetrated my soul. My breath came from deep within me, my arms felt like they could lift a heavy rock. A resolve I'd never had before consumed me. *You can do this; you can stop this abuse. You need to stop this. The truth will set you free.* This was the message that I acted on, yet it came to me without words. I needed to tell the truth and maybe I could stop this abuse from continuing.

I got up from my prayer and stared at my roommate Megan, sleeping peacefully on her little cot-like bed. My mind was infused with the amazing image I had just seen and felt. It still glowed inside me. *I hope she wakes up soon, I need to tell her my plan.*

As soon as I manifested those thoughts Megan woke up. I sat down next to her bed and said, "You know this isn't right. He said you and I were his wives, and now he's trying to seduce Kimaya. I couldn't sleep last night thinking about it. This has to stop. We need to go tell Ma Yogalina; she will know what to do."

Megan's eyes grew wide as I spoke. "I... I... don't know," she said.

"We need to protect Kimaya," I continued, consumed by the conviction that the truth would set us free.

Finally, my conviction penetrated her brainwashing. She nodded her head. She wanted to protect Kimaya too.

"Would you go with me to talk to Ma Yogalina? I think we can trust her to do what is right."

Finally, Megan whispered, "Yes."

"Thanks," I said, praying she wouldn't change her mind.

Although Ma Yogalina had said little as she'd instructed us in hatha yoga each morning, she had taken vows of a monk, so I thought that meant she would be honest. But worried, *Does she know about this? Is she one of his wives too? In any case, she needs to know*. I thought this to myself, I didn't say it to Megan.

We made a private appointment to meet with her after hatha yoga. I concentrated all through class bringing that serene light of Christ into my heart breathing its strength. Megan watched me, and she seemed to gain strength from the presence I carried in my heart.

Megan and I sat cross-legged on the floor below Ma Yogalina. She sat above us in a raised seat appearing perfectly calm, almost enlightened in her orange robe.

"What is it you wish to speak with me about that you couldn't ask in front of the class?"

"Something very private," I answered.

"What is that?" she asked.

"Swami told me that I was his wife in a previous life, and he told Megan that too," I blurted out, straining to keep calm and serene.

"He what?" she asked, shaking her head.

"Did he seduce you?"

"Yes, and Megan too."

"Is this true, Megan?"

Megan nodded her head, her whole-body trembling. I wanted to reach out and hold her.

"And now he is getting ready to seduce Kimaya. I just know it," I said, my voice no longer calm. "She's so young and innocent. I just hate to see this happen to her".

Ma's thin body tensed; her jaw clenched. She said, "We'll just have to see about this," her voice hissing in a controlled anger. She promptly dismissed us and walked out of the room.

"I don't think she believed us. I don't think this was a good idea. Nothing good is going to come out of this." Megan's body was trembling as she spoke to me.

"It is okay; we spoke the truth," I reassured her.

It was just two hours later that I was called for a private audience with the Swami himself. Perhaps I should have been afraid, but I wasn't. I carried the light I'd seen in the mountains in my heart, and Swami Rama seemed to know it. I believed I could make a difference.

He was angry, but his anger had no effect on me.

"How could you do this? Why did you go to Ma Yogalina of all people?

"She seemed to be the one who needed to know. You already knew. You know what you've been doing, so why should I talk to you?"

"You made her faint. You hear? She fainted. How could you do such a thing?"

"I didn't do anything. You did it."

He stopped talking then. He became very quiet. He actually seemed remorseful.

"I've been trying to practice a secret tantra yoga, but now that I've been found out, I will stop. I'm doing lots of good works, the eye hospital...Everything will fall apart if you persist in telling this story. Lots of people will be hurt."

Now that made me stop and think of the bigger picture. *Maybe he was doing something good. He'd gotten a lot of people off drugs. I knew that was true. He'd given some people a positive direction, a purpose in life. If he stops seducing women now, maybe it will be okay and I won't have to talk about this again.*

"How do I know you are really going to stop doing this?" I asked.

"I promise you." And he left the room, returning with a coral ring on a chain in his hand. "I'm giving you this ring as a symbol of my promise," he placed the ring around my neck.

The intense presence of his personality took over my resolve from my prayers. *Maybe I have done some good here. Perhaps he's seen the light, and he will stop abusing women.*

"Okay, I will be silent for now. But if I hear you're doing this again, I will do everything in my power to stop you," I said, looking him straight in the eye.

I walked out with my head held high. Maybe this was why I'd come to India, to stop this.

But after Megan went to see him, she came back looking like a dish rag. She was stooped over, in utter dejection. She didn't see the light that I'd seen, I'd just talked her into it by my conviction. She had sat against him without the light, I should have gone with her.

"We really shouldn't have done that," she whispered, her mouth just barely moving.

"Oh, but he's promised to stop seducing women. That's good news. We did something good," I said still seeing that light that had inspired me. "No, no, I don't think so," she said again. A cloud of darkness clouded over eyes. Her thin body trembled; her beautiful black hair hung listless around a youthful face suddenly lined with sadness.

I took her in my arms, "We said the truth, truth is a good thing," I said, trying to assure her that we were right.

I didn't know what he'd said to her, but my confidence that everything was going to be okay started to erode. I was upset by how he used his power to devastate this sensitive girl. Still, I felt that for now, this was the correct path.

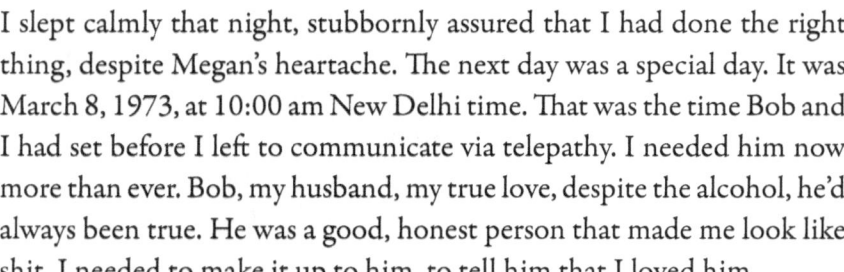

I slept calmly that night, stubbornly assured that I had done the right thing, despite Megan's heartache. The next day was a special day. It was March 8, 1973, at 10:00 am New Delhi time. That was the time Bob and I had set before I left to communicate via telepathy. I needed him now more than ever. Bob, my husband, my true love, despite the alcohol, he'd always been true. He was a good, honest person that made me look like shit. I needed to make it up to him, to tell him that I loved him.

I went up into the dorm room all by myself and sat cross-legged with my spine straight. I cleared my mind of every thought except the air bringing oxygen to every cell of my body. My heart swelled up with love thoughts. In my mind I saw Bob sitting still on the other side of the world. "I love you. I truly love you." I let the air vibrate these thoughts from the breath that seemed to flow out from my heart. "I'm so sorry if I've wronged you. I know you love me, and I love you." I could feel this emotion of love that I was sending to the other side of the world.

I felt his presence in my mind, the sincerity that had joined our youthful bodies and minds. I felt the deep love, and then a desperate longing, questioning, a feeling that I really needed to go home engulfed me. I needed to leave and go home NOW. The feeling was immediate and desperate. I got up from that meditation shaking my head and pacing back and forth in my little room. There was just one more week before I was supposed to go home, yet I wanted to leave NOW.

I sent a note to Swami Rama telling him I needed to leave immediately. Our stay in India had only one more week.

Rather than write an answer, Swami Rama came up to my room. Towering over me, he said,

"Oh no, you can't go. You will miss seeing the Taj Mahal, one of the most beautiful places in the world. You must stay."

He was very adamant that I stay. He must have thought my leaving would raise questions among his followers.

After he left the room, Kimaya turned to me and said, "Oh please stay, we can travel together. You'll miss everything if you leave now."

Kimaya's eyes still glowed. Her reassurance calmed me. She was the one I wanted to save from his grasp, and I hoped I had protected her so she would not be sexually abused. For her I agreed to stay.

The next morning, I took a long walk around the ashram. As I walked through the patio, I stared at the huge potted crown of thorns blooming. Four pink petals surrounded a tiny yellow center, and the flower stalks grew straight out from its thorny stem. My crown of thorns at home in the living room was probably blooming now, too, while the snow was melting outside. I hoped it would still be there when I got home. Further down the path, a servant turned the soil over under the fruit tree. The bare ground would keep snakes from coming up to the ashram. I wandered down to the Ganges; this was the first time I'd left the ashram on my own. The water rushed past on the right. I stumbled over rocks, but I felt free and brave, like a weight had been lifted from my shoulders. At first, I didn't see anyone around. Further in the distance I saw some women in dirty saris crouched down, digging on top of a hill of trash. A little boy hovered near them; his eyes as big as saucers. I approached with my camera and tape recorder. I spoke to them in English and asked to take their pictures. They didn't speak, but their gestures indicated it was okay. I recorded their voices as I asked. "What are you doing?"

They held up small pieces of black crumbly rock, and said, "coal."

I understood they were gathering these small chunks of coal to cook on.

I played the recording back to them. They giggled.

I wished there was some way I could help. If I'd had a Polaroid camera, I could at least have given them a picture of their beautiful son.

The sun was high in the sky as I retraced my steps. I hurried back to the ashram. They'd be serving lunch and probably be missing me. As I approached, I saw a large crowd was gathered in the courtyard around a strange machine. I joined the crowd, Kimaya whispered, "Where have you been?"

"I just went for a walk."

'You almost missed it."

"Missed what?"

They were all drinking a strange, almost clear liquid. The operator put sticks of sugar cane into one end of the press, cranked the handle and a liquid came out of the spout. I stood in line with a glass, they filled it with fresh sugar cane juice. It tasted sweet, but not too sweet, as it slowly passed over my taste buds and down my throat. I sipped, smiling. Staying a little longer was going to be okay.

The next day we all packed our suitcases and headed southwest to Haridwar. Swami Rama waved to the group as we left. It was long ride on the bus, and I was happy to be starting the trip homeward. Haridwar was an ancient city on the banks of the Ganges, the destination for many Hindu pilgrims. We deposited our bags in the hotel and headed down to the Ganges. The sacred river teemed with people everywhere. A man without any legs pushed himself along the street with his arms on a low rolling platform. Everyone ignored him. There were beggars everywhere and we were given strict instructions not to give them anything. How could I help this multitude? Where would I start? I would be overwhelmed. My heart reached out in grief.

Ghat (ancient river landing steps) led down to the water; men in just loin cloths descended them and were submerged in the water, to get healed or have their sins removed. On the walk back we passed a tiny hand-constructed tent with a skinny man sitting outside, his legs crossed in meditation. *Maybe this was a true swami, a wise man beyond the cares of the material world? That is a lot different from Swami Rama,* I thought.

After dinner when the sun had set, we returned to the river. The crowds carried small lanterns. The air sang with rhythmic bells dancing with each step towards the river. People placed their little lantern boats in the water to honor their ancestors or to carry a prayer to the gods. I marveled at everything around me - a world in vivid color and sound. I recorded the bells chiming on my tape recorder.

The next morning early, the servants put the luggage back on the bus, and we rode more than seven hours south to Agra, the city of the Taj Mahal. After a leisurely dinner and a night's rest, in the morning a bus took us to see this wonder of the world. The bus dropped us off a short distance away from the entrance. As soon as I saw it, I had to stop and stand still, staring at its beauty, white marble ascending into the sky. The gardens that start way before it symbolized the crossing over into paradise. Trees border both sides of four reflecting ponds. Roses bloomed along the way. With every step the Taj loomed taller and more magnificent. I had to look away to get my bearings. I was surrounded by tourists from all over the world: Indian Hindu women in beautiful saris, Muslim women with their faces covered by veils, and little girls with brightly colored long tunics and silk pants. I stopped to take a picture of a Muslim woman, she lifted her veil for the picture, a friendly gesture, but I'd wanted to photograph the veil.

I too was wearing a sari. My long red hair flowed down my orange sari with a floral pattern woven into the silk. A young Indian tourist asked in broken English if he could take a picture with me. I nodded my head, yes - after all, I was taking pictures of everyone. I was surprised when he gave the camera to a friend and put his arm around my shoulder, pulling me close. I quickly rejoined my friends, laughing, and said, "I wonder what story he is planning to tell to go with that picture?"

Kimaya, Megan, and I walked up the final steps to the porch platform in silent awe. Now we could see the inlaid green jade and red blood stone vines in the wall. We'd been told some precious stones had been removed, but I couldn't tell what it had looked like centuries ago, just that now it was beautiful.

It amazed me to realize that this was a mausoleum built to honor the emperor's third wife, a wife who bore him fourteen children, and died in childbirth. We took off our shoes and were allowed inside, in silence, no pictures. Inside the tall ceiling echoed every sound. This tomb was indeed one of the wonders of the world, but I still longed to be home as soon as possible.

Our final meal in India was in a very fancy restaurant. My lips quivered in anticipation when I saw the tall glasses of ice water at each setting. I hadn't had any ice water for a month. Besides while in India I'd been careful to have tea or boiled water because the water might contain pathogens my body wasn't used to. When I sat down to dinner, I took a big sip of that cool clear water. Big mistake.

The next day, flying on the plane home, we all had diarrhea from drinking the water in the restaurant. There was a constant line of desperate people standing at the back of the plane. And when I finally got into the tiny toilet, the smell of putrid curry almost made me puke. They kept feeding us vegetarians the same curry until the next day. When the plane finally landed in England, we were greeted by British scones and cheese. We all wanted to start clapping, relieved to have some different food. I was too tired and sick to get off and explore the airports. Of course, we had to get off in New York and go through customs, then on to Chicago. I rushed in the middle of the night to catch my plane to Minneapolis.

It was early morning when Bob greeted me as I came down the gangway into the airport. His welcome hug was strange and stiff, the smile on his face was forced, but I was too tired to question it. Bob helped me get our luggage in the car, and I collapsed into a jet-lagged coma.

CHAPTER 9

Aftermath at Home
1973

THE NEXT MORNING, I struggled to open my eyes as the bed wobbled. *What? What's going on?* My brain was still asleep. I rolled over on my back and the bed rolled back and forth. *Where am I?* I remembered flying through the air trying to sleep in uncomfortable airplane seats, but this was nothing like that. I jerked again and the bed sloshed under me. Then it finally registered, *I'm home. This is our waterbed I'm floating upon.*

I slowly rolled on the confined water. It rolled with me. I tried to reach the edge of the bed. This was the cheapest type of waterbed, just a wooden frame placed on the floor, with a plastic mattress filled with water. A heater underneath the bed kept the water from being cold. Getting out was nearly impossible. When I reached the edge, I grabbed the wooden frame and tossed one leg onto the floor. My other leg plunged down into the water mattress while I struggled to swing the rest of myself upright. My exhausted brain let my body fall face down back into the sloshing mattress. I grabbed my pillow to use as a floatation device to keep my head up, while my mind descended back into sleep. I would have slept the entire day, but my bladder screamed it was time to get up. Sleeping on a bladder of water was okay, laying in pee was not. I raised my body up so I was balanced on my hands and knees. I crawled very slowly to the edge of the bed, once again grabbed the wooden frame. This time I swung my legs, so I was seated with both feet on the floor. Swinging my arms up, I straightened my bent knees; finally upright, I ran to the bathroom.

When I got out of the bathroom, I blinked at the bright light streaming in from the bank of windows overlooking Coon Lake. Bright yellow-green blades of grass were springing up everywhere. It was mid-March. The snow had melted during the month I was gone.

I smiled; my favorite season had arrived. "Bob, Bob, where are you?" I yelled out. I wanted to run and jump in his arms and give him a big hug. I was home; I was safe.

"I'm here," a soft hoarse voice whispered.

As I was standing by the windows, in our small house I could see him in the kitchen. His back was turned toward me, and he was getting his coffee started. I couldn't see his face.

"Are you sick?" I asked, concerned by the guttural sound of his voice. I walked over to give him a hug. He pushed me away.

"Not now."

I was shocked. Never in the six years we'd been married had he refused a hug.

I sat down across the table from where he was standing next to the coffee pot. The jet lag I woke up with had suddenly disappeared.

I stared up at him as he continued to fidget with the coffee maker, his eyes avoiding mine. "What's the matter? I love you," I said, letting my mouth turn down in a sad pout that had always made him melt.

"I'm not so sure," he said, refusing to look at me.

"Did you get the telepathic message I sent you?"

"Yes, yes, I think I did. That was what gave me hope. I sat here; at that time we'd picked. I just felt love coming from you."

I remembered that day when I sat and sent thoughts out to him. "I felt you too, and I felt that you wanted me to come right home. I tried to arrange it so I could come home a week earlier, but it didn't work out."

He shoved a crumpled piece of paper in my hand.

"What's this?" I asked. He hadn't given me time to grab the paper, and it dropped slowly to the floor.

"You tell me what it is." Anger flashed in his blue eyes.

I bent down to retrieve the paper smoothing its crinkled surface. I read the last sentence, "I'm coming to study yoga, and I want to be sure that we will not be getting together for anything intimate again." *My God, it was the rough draft of the note I'd written Swami Rama before I left.*

My chest felt tight; a deep sadness surrounded me. "I'm sorry I didn't come home sooner. I'm really sorry. I do love you; I really do," I said, thinking of his sincere love for me, wondering if he'd ever forgive me.

He looked at me. His eyes filled with confined tears, like the water in the waterbed, they didn't escape, or flow down his cheeks. He kept his emotions in check. They stayed, pooled in the corners of his eyes.

"I found the letter in your desk. I just didn't know what to think," he said.

I gulped. My head spun; the world I'd carefully built was crumbling. I wanted to crawl down into a deep, deep hole and never come out. I remembered when he proposed to me. He'd held me and said, "I want to take care of you forever." He was my rock; I always knew he'd meant what he said. His love for me was beyond question, unlike my own.

I opened my mouth to explain, then shut it, unable to say a word. Minutes passed as I sat with my head down, knowing I needed to tell him what had happened in India. I'd promised not to tell, but he needed to know,

"I was really, really stupid. Swami Rama had me convinced that I was his wife from a past life. I believed him. He seduced me when I went to Topeka, Kansas. I wanted to be sure in India I'd be staying just as a student. I didn't want to be his wife in this life. In India I met another girl he'd told the same story to. I still like Arya and yoga, but I don't want anything to do with Swami Rama," I said, trying to set the record straight.

But it wasn't straight, nothing was straight. My whole life was bent out of shape.

Bob wanted to believe me. He walked around the table towards me, and I stood up, my head still down. He took me in his arms and held me in a tight embrace. I wasn't sure if it was a hold of forgiveness, or a hold of anger and possession. He didn't say anything more. It wasn't his way.

I didn't tell anyone else about what happened, not with Swami Rama nor with Bob and me. I withdrew from any activities at the meditation temple without saying why. I went to work at my new job teaching at Woodbury Junior High School. Sometimes I drove the hour commute in my own car, other days Bob and I commuted together. He worked downtown doing employment security research for the state. I picked him up in the city after my day of teaching and we came home. As soon as we walked through the door Bob grabbed a can of beer from the fridge and sat down to relax.

I made up the dinner I'd planned over the weekend. Vegetarian cooking was complicated. There weren't any veggie burgers for sale in the grocery store in the 1970s. I planned the weekday meals out in advance over the weekend, often precooking parts and putting them in the freezer for workdays. Bob occasionally vacuumed, and did his own ironing, but otherwise I did all of the housework, including washing the dishes. We didn't talk about yoga or my experience in India. I tried to be the perfect wife. I thought through my actions, maybe Bob would forgive me.

Two months later I received a strange phone call from one of Arya's assistants at the Meditation Center. "There is an important election on May 6, for the Meditation Temple that you should attend. I hope you can come." It sounded like they were almost begging me to come.

"I'm not sure. I'm very busy."

There was no way that I was going to attend this meeting. What was it anyway? I wondered. My hand shook as I set down the telephone receiver.

I'd not been able to meditate since I'd returned from India. Prior to that, I'd sat in relaxed meditation at least thirty minutes every day. Now, when I closed my eyes and attempted to meditate while concentrating on my breath, instead of relaxing my whole body tensed up in fear. It felt that instead of opening my mind up to God, I was opening a door for Swami Rama. I was afraid that if I were to descend into a deep meditative state Swami Rama would be able to read my mind and maybe even control me.

The election meeting came and went, and I didn't attend. No one called, but I got a copy of the minutes in the mail. I puzzled over them reading and rereading them. My friends from the University, Dr. Neville Woolf (Nick) and Dr Roger Jones had resigned as president and vice president of the center. *Did they know about Swami Rama practicing tantra?* It quoted Arya as saying, "A yoga center in any deep tradition has an essential requirement of certain disciplines. It is wrong to give those disciplines the name of religion or culture." That meant *they left because Arya was insisting on too many Hindu rituals, and they didn't know about the tantra shit.*

I decided to call Nick's wife Patricia Woolf who was a psychologist and a close friend. Nick and Patricia had met at the Meditation Center, and Swami Rama had told Nick to marry Patricia. Arya married them in a Hindu wedding ceremony, so their leaving was a big deal. I needed to find out what was really happening.

"Hi, this is Pat from the Meditation Center. I haven't been there since I came back from India in March. I just heard that you guys left"

"Yes, it's a complicated story. I actually wrote a letter of resignation to the executive committee, Arya and Swami Rama to explain my position. The Temple and Arya in particular has been controlling people through guilt. Let me find it and read it to you." I waited while Patricia retrieved the letter, "The Temple produces dependent people afraid to disagree with THE TEACHINGS - or the guru for fear of blasphemy. Swamiji (Swami Rama) is understood to be some semi-divine figure in whose presence one quakes and is tongue-tied, who knows one's very thought (even from a distance), who peers deeply into one when one is lucky enough to see him, who foresees one's future, who must be implicitly obeyed."

Hearing that made me realize how Arya's teachings had set me up for Swami Rama's advances. I didn't think he'd meant to do it, and I still kept my mouth shut.

"I've been feeling the same way," I said, struggling to keep calm as my eyes filled with tears. Just hearing someone else verify my feelings was a great relief.

"Nick and I, and Roger and another friend have been meeting on Sundays at Roger's house. We are studying the teachings of an American guru, who lives in Taos, New Mexico, Herman Rednick. Would you and Bob like to join us? It's a potluck."

"I'll have to ask Bob, but I'd love to come, I need a group." I hoped meeting with like-minded people studying under a different teacher would allow me to meditate again. I wasn't really interested in another guru, but it would be wonderful to get together, to be able to return to my practice and find my own sacred place. If Bob was willing to come with me it might help us get back on the same page.

As soon as I got off the phone, I went to Bob to ask him about it, I was careful not to use the word guru. I said, "Nick and Patricia and Roger have left the Meditation Center too. They've invited us to join them next Sunday for a potluck." I was sure we'd learn more about the meditation part when we got to their house.

"Sure, that sounds fine," Bob said. He liked and respected both Roger and Nick, especially since they were professors at the university.

The next Sunday, I made my favorite quiche and we drove into the city to Roger Jones's home. Nick and his friend brought over a lesson and a Mandala-like drawing that had been drawn by Herman Rednick. Herman was an artist who taught his own meditation technique and did not charge for his lessons, so we felt maybe he was for real. He specialized in developing relationships between married couples and expanding this love through the group to all people. Being accepted as part of a group no matter how small was very important for both of us.

While we were enjoying my quiche and the delicious salad Pat had made, Bob said, "My latest analysis indicates that airlines are a good investment right now." It was off the topic, but it turned out to be very relevant small talk.

Everyone turned towards him. They knew Bob did economic planning and even astronomers were interested in making good investments.

"Why is that?" Roger asked.

Bob continued analyzing current trends. I admired his intellectual thinking, but I missed the chanting and group meditation at the center. At least here I wasn't living a lie, even if I wasn't telling the group why I'd left the Meditation Center.

We went to Roger's house almost every Sunday for the next year. We would meditate together on a drawing that Herman Rednick sent to the group.

To separate myself from the fear of Swami Rama that meditation generated, I created my own self-affirmation mantra. I sat in the lotus posture, my legs crossed and my back straight. As I breathed in, I thought, *I like myself as an expression of the life force.* The words were garbled and didn't sing correctly, but it calmed me to reach out to the idea of a universal life force.

I'd formed such a strong bond with my roommates from India and I wanted to reach out to them and make sure they were okay. I'd planned to visit Megan at her home in Madison in July, but I had to cancel at the last minute. I don't remember what I wrote to her, but I must have described how I'd left the Meditation Center. I saved the letter she wrote back all these years. To this day I find it disturbing to read. She'd shared my concern for Kimaya, and described her feelings graphically:

"The hard fish to swallow, the fish-bone lodged in the throat, has been the same things that bothered you; Swami's refusal to tell honestly what was happening with Kimaya. The times I get to thinking about it, I get really upset."

Okay, that was my concern too, but what she said next made me afraid for her, myself and the world. She wrote, "In any case, he is so powerful, he's going to do what he wants no matter what, and it would just be a waste of vital life force to try to comprehend or control his actions."

Is that what the world should say about those who abuse power? I didn't think so. I did not believe he was that powerful. We were the ones, his followers - we were the ones who gave him power.

September 5, 1973, I received a letter from the girl I'd wanted to save from being seduced by Swami Rama. Her letter was full of the joy that was Kimaya. She mentioned that she hadn't seen me at the Meditation Center and described a wonderful camping trip in northern Minnesota. The last paragraph of the letter said, "I bet you've wondered what happened between me and Swami after the big crisis in India? Well, nothing exciting. Swamiji never mentioned it again to me. And our relationship changed and grew. And I've learned so much from him. I've felt a lot stronger since India, a lot more independent." I read and reread that paragraph feeling relieved. From that statement I was grateful, believing Swami Rama had actually kept his promise to me and hadn't continued to have sexual relations with women.

That fall, in addition to teaching junior high school during the day, I taught a yoga class in the evenings at a local public school. I developed a curriculum for my class without any reference to the guru idea. We practiced deep breathing, and basic yoga postures. I ended with the class lying down, almost falling asleep, as I guided them into a state of deep relaxation.

Bob and I celebrated seven years of marriage. We owned a house, and we both had good jobs. My biological clock was blaring in my ears; I desperately wanted a baby. Looking for some guidance outside of ourselves we turned to consulting the I Ching. The I Ching was an ancient Chinese oracle, so I asked the I Ching, "What is the state of the child so longed for and so often put off?" I wrote this down in my diary and concentrated on the question as I tossed three coins. The heads or tails of the coins were converted into calculation, each toss indicating the shape of one line of a present hexagram. All the lines were changed to their opposites to create the future hexagram. In this ancient Chinese text, the only thing constant is change, therefore your prediction changes. Once I had the hexagram, I looked it up in our copy of *The Book of Changes*. The book said my present hexagram represented contented joyousness, and its future configuration was good future. I ran to Bob and showed it to him.

"That's nice," he said without enthusiasm. He'd agreed not to practice birth control, but I wasn't so sure if he was really happy about it. It seemed like he was only happy riding his BMW motorcycle or going to the bar. I was constantly worried, that he'd have an accident or get another DWI.

One day in May, Bob called saying, "I don't think I'll make it home for dinner." I was glad that at least he'd called. At midnight, still he wasn't home, then it was 1:30 and I crawled into bed by myself. At 3:30 a.m. I woke up feeling a heavy body on top of me breathing rancid beer breath into my nose in a drunken attempt at sex. I turned, pushed him off and turned my back to him. I wanted to vomit at the smell of him. This disgusting creature was not the husband I'd married.

The next day, I woke up exhausted and rushed off to work. When he sobered up the next day, I told him I couldn't have my sleep interrupted like that and go to work. He said, "I'm sorry, I don't remember doing that."

I didn't understand why he couldn't remember, but I forgave him.

CHAPTER 10

The Letters
1974

A YEAR PASSED, Bob tried to control his drinking, and we attended weekly Sunday potlucks with Nick and Roger, at Roger's home. Then in December 1974 the phone rang. I picked up the receiver to hear the voice of my dear friend Debbie. She and her husband, Phil, had been part of the group that started the Meditation Center. I hadn't told her anything, but I'm sure she must have noticed that I wasn't coming to the Meditation Center anymore.

"Have you heard from Shanti or Dan?" she asked.

"No, not since they went to India," I said.

Shanti was the embodiment of the Indian name Arya had given her. I didn't know her very well but her very presence brought "peace", the Sanskrit meaning of her name. I remembered seeing her before I went to India. Her eyes glowed when Arya announced she'd been chosen to study in India. As I'd watched her then, standing in the back of Arya's attic just one month after my seduction by Swami Rama, I worried, *Is he going to seduce her too?* I dismissed it, thinking *No he was just my husband from a previous life, that's all.* Just to be sure I gave her a going-away card that said, "I hope that your experience proves to be a totally spiritual one." Somehow, I thought this could be translated as a subtle warning.

The next year Shanti came back from India and Swami Rama arranged for her to marry Dan. That made me feel assured that Swami Rama was actually teaching her in India and hadn't seduced her. Dan was a brilliant young man who was working on his PhD in Sanskrit. He was so sincere and generous that he was even teaching the yoga students Sanskrit. Sanskrit was the language of the ancient Indian texts that held the answers to life's secrets. According to Arya there were words in Sanskrit that could not be translated. I'd learned French and Japanese, but my mind refused to learn Sanskrit. I was in awe of Dan; he wouldn't have been duped by a fake Swami. I thought Shanti and Dan had a perfect marriage blessed by Swami Rama, and Arya.

Debbie continued, "I just got a long letter from Shanti and one from Dan just arrived, I think you should read them." She seemed to know something I didn't know. *Did she suspect something about me?*

"Sure, but what is it about?" I answered, totally confused. *Why would they be sending letters that I should read?* I thought, remembering that now after they'd married, they'd both gone back to India to work at Swami Rama's ashram.

"I think you should come over and read the letters," she repeated.

I really didn't want to be part of the Meditation Center any more, but Debbie was more than a member of the center, she was a friend. The next weekend I drove to her apartment.

As I entered their apartment, I felt the warmth of our close friendship when she offered me a cup of tea. Her husband, Phil, hovered in the background, wanting to see what was happening, but not sitting down with us.

"I'm so glad you came over. I just don't know what to do with this letter," Debbie said

I took a sip of my tea, as Debbie brought me a letter written in tiny handwriting on an airmail envelope.

The letter was dated 2 December 1974. I squinted to read the minuscule handwriting. It wasn't addressed just to Debbie; the salutation read "Dear friends."

My heart sank, as the letter detailed my worst nightmare. In it Shanti wrote that ever since her first personal appointment with Swami Rama in April 1971, she had been his lover.

That would have been just after he seduced me in March of 1971. *No wonder he dropped me. He'd found Shanti*, I thought, thankful that I had been dropped.

Shanti went on to describe many experiences similar to mine. Instead of Vivekananda, she'd read the Autobiography of a Yogi by Yogananda, so she had been sure that when she was ready, the guru would appear. Using this preparation to his advantage, Swami Rama also told her how "he'd been waiting for her". I had to suppress a laugh when I read it. She thought maybe she would be put into Samadhi by having sex with an enlightened guru. "Only I wasn't," she'd added.

He had used the same line on Shanti that he'd used on me. "You are the only one I've ever had sex with in this life." And of course, she was not to tell anyone.

Oh, weren't we gullible? I thought.

When Shanti had second thoughts, she went to Arya, telling him she had doubts about her guru Swami Rama. She wasn't sure she wanted to devote her life to him.

Arya spent hours assuring her that "the ways of a realized person are very strange indeed, and everything he says and does has great meaning, and the guru is constantly working for his disciple's improvement."

With that explanation firmly implanted in her mind Shanti went on to follow her guru lover, bowing to his every whim. She didn't talk to him much because why should she since he knew her thoughts and needs.

As I read this, I realized this could have been me, if I hadn't made demands of him, or if I hadn't been married. I might have been the girl servicing him in India.

Shanti described living in India with him - he was abusive, on the rare occasions when he paid any attention to her at all. When her visa ended, she returned to America and fell in love with Dan. Swami Rama was still her guru, and she wouldn't do anything against his will, so she and Dan asked Swami Rama for permission to marry and he granted it. Dan of course never knew that his girlfriend had been the "celibate" Swami Rama's lover.

Dan and Shanti as newlyweds went back to work at Swami Rama's ashram in India. Shanti was still devoted to Swami Rama and wanted to continue to practice yoga under him. Swami Rama put them in separate sleeping quarters saying that brahmacharya (abstinence) was the rule in the ashram. This made Dan feel guilty, thinking perhaps he and Shanti had failed their guru by not being celibate. While Dan spent time in one room working on a paper, Swami Rama was going to present at an upcoming international yoga conference. Swami Rama was forcing Shanti to have sex with him in another part of the ashram.

Shanti became very distraught and prayed for guidance. She started going off on her own. In the town of Rishikesh she met a yogi called Baba, who had no possessions and slept in a cave. She confided her confusion to him. He told her, "Pray, listen to your heart, and love God."

She listened and saw Swami Rama for what he was: a greedy, selfish person who cared only for himself, and if he ever did practice yoga in his life, he was one of those who had fallen from the path.

Shanti stayed with some women who lived near Baba, and planned to leave Swami Rama's ashram, but decided this wasn't fair to Dan. So, she went back and told Dan what had been going on between her and Rama.

Dan was shocked. He believed her, but also knew from his study of the Vedas how improper this behavior was. For a guru to do this with his disciple was incest of the worst order, and then to have done this with the wife of a man who was devoting himself to Swami Rama, working for him, writing things for the Himalayan Institute, was more than he could bear. He left the same day without Shanti, not sure where he was going, or telling anyone why.

The letter went on to describe how she went back to the ashram to confront Swami Rama. He tried to use guilt and offers of enlightenment to get her to take back what she had told Dan and get back on the path. "You will regret this your whole life," he told her.

Shanti held the image of Baba in her mind and saw the light. Baba's friends said that they would protect her, and that Swami Rama. could not harm her.

Shanti went to Delhi and found Dan. They got back together, traveling, and studying in India. After hearing other stories in India about Rama's transgressions they decided to share their story with friends at the Meditation Center. This letter was written just to friends, and they didn't want wild rumors floating around, but felt we needed to know.

Before I had a chance to respond, Debbie immediately placed another letter in front of me. This one was from Dan.

Dan's letter was a scathing rejection of Swami Rama and a heart-rending account of his betrayal by Shanti. It brought tears to my eyes. I felt the pain that Bob must have felt when he found the letter I wrote. When I finished reading, I felt rage. I wanted to scream, at the world, at myself. *I'd seen the light, but I didn't listen, did I? I believed Swami Rama when he said he would stop doing this.* I remembered my promise to him, "If I hear you are continuing to do this, I will do everything in my power to stop you." Now I needed to do just that.

I looked up at Debbie, my heart heavy. I didn't need to keep secrets any longer. "You probably suspected that I too was one of his victims. He seduced me in March of 1971 after a lecture at the Unity Village in Topeka Kansas. I was on my way home from doing research for my thesis at the Menninger Research Foundation"

I blurted out the confession, feeling sick to my stomach. This was much worse than I'd ever imagined.

"What can we do to stop this?" Debbie asked.

"I think we start by telling the truth to anyone who will listen," I said, and Debbie agreed.

Debbie hadn't been one of his victims, but we were sure there were others. I talked to more women and discovered that he'd unsuccessfully tried to seduce my friend, Alice. When Swami Rama tried to seduce her, she'd laughed in his face. I still respected Arya and thought that if Alice and I went together to talk to Arya, maybe he'd come to his senses and disassociate the Meditation Center in Minneapolis from Swami Rama. It could be its own separate thing, not associated with the Himalayan Institute. Then I could feel safe returning to my participation in the Meditation Center, which I'd loved.

Dan mentioned in his letter that he thought, if this came out in America, Arya might commit suicide because he was so devoted to Swami Rama. But I had known him before he met Swami Rama. He had been a very decent person and I was sure he'd listen to us.

Alice and I made an appointment to speak to him together. We walked in and sat down on the floor in front of Arya, who was seated cross-legged with his back perfectly straight on a large pillow. He was dressed in his comfortable Indian clothes with a shawl draped over his shoulder.

"What is it you want to tell me?" he asked, his eyes soft and kind as always.

"We thought you should know what has been going on," I said.

"What do you mean, going on?" Arya questioned.

"Well, Swami Rama has been seducing women," I answered.

"That's impossible, Swami Rama is celibate," he answered, his eyes turning cold, glaring at me.

I had trouble speaking, but Alice took over. "I met him in New York. He said he was overjoyed to see me, and that he had been waiting for me for a long time. Then he proceeded to kiss me and tell me that I was his one and only. I pushed him away. I said, "I'm looking for a guru, not a lover." He looked very hurt, like he couldn't believe I'd turned him down.

"He seduced me at the Unity Village in Topeka, Kansas", I added. "But unfortunately, I was not as wise as Alice." Arya shook his head, like he was blocking this information from penetrating the outside of his ears.

"You are totally wrong. I never want to see you inside this temple again. If you come here, I will be sure that you are removed." With that, we were excommunicated.

Alice and I walked proudly out the door, sad to have bothered to tell the truth to a brick wall.

At home, I shared what had happened with Bob. I tried to figure it out. Arya had been like a father to me; I felt betrayed. It was a new death, like when my real father had died.

Why had he done this? Was he a monster too?

Bob interrupted my story telling and said, "Remember, when I first met Swami Rama; I told you he was no good."

"Yes, I do remember that," I said.

"I couldn't tell you why, but I just felt it."

Bob had a way of judging people's character, which he followed all of his life.

Arya didn't believe me, but maybe someone would. My friends Debbie and Phil, Pat and Nick Woolf and other founding members of the Meditation Center certainly believed my story along with the letters that Shanti and Dan wrote. We'd been together since the beginning of the Meditation Center. We'd gone to meetings and classes in Arya's attic, helped with the retreats and helped find the building where Arya was living, and the Meditation Center was located.

My first impulse was to tell the Andersons, Valerie, and her husband Tad. They were both graduate students working on their PhDs in biochemistry. They'd just relocated to Philadelphia to be close to the Himalayan Institute that Swami Rama was creating there. I thought they really needed to know about this. We'd been friends in the psychology group, and I'd been to their home in Minnesota. I wrote the letter on December 20th.

My friend Valerie received my letter on Christmas Day. She wrote back asking, *"How dare you ruin my Christmas with this garbage?"* It was the angriest letter I ever received in my life. I felt my hands burning as I held her reply. Her anger made my blood boil, and she wrote that her husband thought we were being prudish. The words of my reply exploded off my pen:

If Swami Rama had told me he wanted to see me to 'make love' or fuck me, it would have been a different situation. However, he used his position as guru to seduce me. As Arya put it, a guru-disciple relationship is a father-daughter relationship, and this is therefore incest. Does Tad reject the description of this as incest and claim it to be just my sexual prudery? It makes me angry, angry at the fucking world, angry at the abuse of women!

I mailed my answer, but I never heard from these friends again. I hoped they disassociated themselves from the Himalayan Institute, but I have no idea whether they did or not.

Dan wrote another letter addressed *Dear Folks,* in which he explained how he was able to forgive Shanti and start over with just the two of them, because he saw Swami Rama as the father who exploited his daughter. Dan stated *"Arya would claim that a realized man can get away with murder. This is a distortion as anyone's common sense will immediately tell him."* Then he quoted an ancient Hindu text, the Vedanta-sara: *"If a realized man does whatever he might, in taking in what is impure, what is the difference between the liberated in life and the lowest dog? The liberated does as he wishes, but never, and this is the point - wishes to do anything harmful to others."* ... In his own words Dan writes,

"Can you imagine an enlightened man instructing his female devotees to lock the door, pull the curtains and say "Lift up your sari?"

The letter continued with some suggestions about what we could do:

Somebody do one thing soon. Please go to the IRS and complain that a lot of taxable dollars have been going untaxed out of the country for years, into the Swiss bank account of his Holiness Swami Rama. I have just read that an agreement has been signed permitting US officials to inspect the accounts of those suspected of cheating the US government. This may be the easiest way to stop Swami Con. See the local man and also the man in Chicago. A complaint should also be made to the Chicago police and the FBI that S.R. is involved in what is jocularly known as 'bunco' or suspected of it. Also practicing medicine without a license. Do press the income tax thing. If it stopped Al Capone, it could well get our fellow. In no case will you be required to provide evidence personally - simply state your suspicions as effectively as possible. If I were back there, I would not let anyone else do it for me. But as I'm over here, I urge someone to take on the task before he flies off to Switzerland to spread his personal brand of enlightenment to that territory.

Please ask Pat, or someone else in the psychiatry business, just what our chances are of getting an involuntary commitment to a mental institution for S.R. Also ask her to contact the Greens in Topeka and ask their advice in interpreting the problem and coping with it. It has struck me that the Greens have something less than reverence for their famous test case.

As I read it during our meeting at Debbie's house, I felt its anger and strength surge through my being. Maybe we could stop Swami Rama. I wrote to Dr. Elmer Green and Dr. Alicia Green at the Menninger Research Foundation. That was where Swami Rama had amazed western scientists by his ability to stop his heartbeat while in a meditative state. Since I had visited them and knew them. I agreed with Dan. *They are such kind and decent people, surely they will help us stop this monster they'd unknowingly helped create.*

This was not what I wanted to be doing. I'd wanted to be a scientist studying the inner workings of the mind and the spirit, and instead I was writing about absolute trash. I'd been trashed and I just wanted to stop other people from being trashed, used, and thrown away like bloody tampons. I started writing, and my hand shook, I scribbled the date January 24, 1975, and then tried to do the salutation. *Dear Dr. Green* on the page and then scratched it out. *Okay I can write Dear Dr. Green,* he won't be mad like the Andersons, or would he? He'd invited me to do research there and taken me into his home. *What if he responds like Arya?* I thought. *So, what, then, he's a jerk too.* I soldiered on, writing the truth. The biblical phrase came to mind, "The truth will set you free." This time I was very careful to include references to other people, people the Greens may have met. Only after describing all of these other people who had left the Meditation Center did I relate my experience of having been seduced by Swami Rama at Unity Village after my visit to them in March of 1971, three years earlier. I folded up all six pages and sent them off.

In February I received a welcome answer. I opened it and scanned my eyes across the Menninger Foundation Letterhead

Dear Pat, it began. At least he didn't seem to be angry like the Andersons. He went on to describe additional women in Honolulu, San Diego and San Francisco. *Good grief, was there no end to this?*

Dr. Green thanked me for sharing this information and he even said he would discuss it with Dr. Arya.

But in his last paragraph he said this was just for learning. He said the past was unimportant. There was no mention about being willing to help us stop this sexual predator, no sense of real indignation in the letter.

Dear Pat:

Thank you for your letter of 24 January about episodes and vicissitudes in the search for Truth. Your letter parallels what several women (from Honolulu to San Diego to San Francisco, etc.) had already told us.

Alyce and I thank you for sharing this information. It solidifies my feeling that I must be very careful to not be responsible in any way for encouraging other people, especially women, to be too trusting. The old saying, "Handsome is, as handsome does" is still true. When possible I will try to discuss these and other problems with Dr. Arya. I see no reason why the doctors in Minneapolis and St. Paul should not know. Perhaps it would help them.

Only one more comment. Experience is for learning and for moving upward. Your perspective is increased, Truth still exists, humans have problems, but we all live in the "here and now" and move forward based on what we have learned. The past is unimportant, only what we do now is of significance. Best wishes for rapid progress on the Path.

Sincerely Yours,

Elmer E. Green

I felt both validated and abandoned. I could tell Dr. Green saw this as a problem, but it wasn't his problem and I felt he thought it wasn't really that important.

CHAPTER 11

Responses to the Letters 1974

I WROTE TO SHANTI asking her if she remembered the card, I'd given her that said, "I hope that your experience proves to be a totally spiritual one," the year she left for India the first time.

A letter written on onion skin airmail paper in her tiny handwriting came back right away. It began, "Yes, I remember your Christmas card some three or four years ago. That seems so far away and yet what was happening at that time has had such a profound effect on me for many years."

As I read her letter I thought, *Oh, if I'd only been honest, been explicit, maybe things wouldn't have been so sad.* Her letter echoed my thoughts. "Had I only said something then there wouldn't have been so many go down after me, but then, given the nature of devotees such as Arya, it wouldn't have made much difference. Arya is always saying he is the instrument of his guru. He certainly is - think of the many young women he has roped in for Rama - like a pimp. Thank God, for every one of us who has managed to escape by whatever means."

I was right there with her on the page. Just like Shanti, I wanted to stop Rama, "once and for all, at whatever the cost." Just like me, she hoped Kimaya had seen the light too, but we didn't know, as I hadn't talked to her for a couple of years now. We both felt if one or two or 10 people are "saved" from Rama, it was worth it.

While Dan and Shanti were in India, another Sanskrit graduate student - Ron, and his wife Indriani - were there too. They were attending a Hindu Festival and heard Shanti had gone "crazy" and Dan was divorcing her. At first, they believed the rumors but decided since Dan was in Kashmir and they were there too, they needed to hear their side of the story.

To their surprise they discovered that Dan and Shanti weren't divorced. When Indriani heard the story, she had to tell her own. She too had been quiet, believing she was the only one.

She was traveling in India when Swami Rama met and wrote to her begging her to come and be a disciple and his secretary. Indriani went to his ashram and when she arrived, he said to her, "I went to see my guru and he said, 'it is necessary for you to undergo sex with me for purification." She believed him implicitly as he made her feel he was doing it out of great sacrifice. She thought perhaps this was complete surrender to the guru as was emphasized in the teachings.

I wanted to laugh and cry out loud. For Megan and me, he was our husband from a different life; to Shanti and Kimaya he was teaching them, and for Indriani it was her purification. He certainly did a bit of shapeshifting, to accomplish his seductions. We were all so gullible. It was nice to know I wasn't alone in my stupidity.

Despite our clamoring, the followers of Swami Rama were ready to go to great lengths to shut us up and assure the other members that we were just nuts. A special meeting was called for February 14, 1974. Arya was called to come to the Meditation Temple and explain to the devotees how we were all crazy. Then there were threats of lawsuits. Then, just as Indriani was arriving in the States and the meeting was taking place, we received this letter signed "Doug". The letter's salutation was:

Welcome Home Baby

Doug carried on about how reputable Rama was, for he'd traveled with him everywhere, but never gave a return address or his name. Then the letter turned nasty, and he said:

Indriani had been traveling around S.E. Asia with a hippie group and slept with anyone she met on the street. As for Shanti he said, *"When she stayed at Rama's ashram she would sneak out at night through the bathroom and disturb the servants, so they found out where she went. It is a well-known fact in Rishikesh that she would go around with anyone for a few rupees. To verify this, I have letters from Nelmai police officers and others. Later she was thrown out of the place where she had stayed*

My eyes burned and my teeth clenched as I whispered to myself "What a lie." As if that wasn't enough, it went on.

Indriani and Shanti were questioned by the Delhi police for exchanging money on the black market. I have letters to verify this. They also say it is not humanly possible for Rama to sleep with such a militant ugly girl like Indriani.

Ugly? From what I'd seen of her she was very beautiful.

There was more.

These girls were staying in Delhi with Dr. Arya's friends. How ungrateful to take advantage and abuse the hospitality of poor Indian people.

I know that these two girls are having marital problems and that they are nymphomaniacs. I know at least 10 boys here in Minneapolis who have slept with Shanti both before and after her marriage.

Another lie.

It is a problem for their husbands to control them and that is why they are thinking of getting rid of them.

"Is this written by an Indian man? No American would write about the husband controlling his wife?" My mind kept wondering who might have written this. The letter went on and on, spouting nonsense ad nauseam. Mainly it was about Shanti and Indriani, but suddenly I saw my name added to the mix. I was listed as one of many confused people in Arya's organization:

This confusion is created by a few confused people such as Debbie, who is having marital problems, I understand, but also Sharon, Veena and Pat. These women have approached Mr. Rama and are perhaps paying him back for being jilted

I certainly did not want to pay him back for being jilted.

Anyone that believes that Mr. Rama had anything to do with Indriani and Shanti really has no brains in their skull. Such people as this do not deserve to be convinced.

If Mr. S. Rama believes in free sex, I am going to kill the son of a bitch. But rest assured I am also going to kill these women who are coming out with such lies.

I was afraid in India. Did I need to be afraid in my own country too?

Again, I assure you that if any part of your letter comes true, I will take severe action against Mr. S. Rama and promised to kill him if it is true. But if it is not true then you should be fully prepared for the consequences, as I am going to do it to you...

Please wait patiently for the genuine story to continue to be found out.

Yours sincerely

Doug

This *Doug* had trouble putting his thought in order, but threats like these were no joke. Greg and Indriani, Dan and Shanti were still in India, but they wrote a letter to the FBI outlining four reasons why the alien who calls himself His Holiness Swami Rama should be deported and not allowed back into the United States. Dan and Greg were both PhD students and they went to great lengths to make their case.

In the 1970's the seduction of women by men in power was not a great concern, but narcotics were. That was listed as the first reason Swami Rama should be deported. "Rama has procured and posted psychedelic drugs and in a public lecture admitted openly to administering LSD to an unsuspecting victim."

Tom, a member of the Meditation Center, told Shanti and wrote an open letter testifying that he had obtained psychedelic drugs on more than one occasion for Rama, even though Rama constantly lectured against the use of any drugs. It was conjectured that he used these drugs in the initiation of his advanced students. The descriptions that Arya and others gave of their initiations closely resembled an LSD or psilocybin trip. Tom ended his open letter saying, "Now I hear he wants to stay in this country as a professional holy man. I feel he is an evil thing, expertly adept at the sham and the lie and the cruel exploitation of gentle people. I give testimony against him, if truth has any measure of weight against money." Tom signed this letter and included his address at the time. He'd known Shanti and admired her as one of those trusting gentle people, but he wasn't gentle. Rama had given him a pair of holy sandals. Tom shot them full of holes and mailed them to Arya to show what he thought of their holy shit.

The second reason they listed for Rama to be deported was sexual immorality, based on his using his spiritual authority to seduce women, and to rape Shanti after she was married.

The third reason was fraudulent money dealings. They listed numerous situations where he acquired donations, saying he was giving them to charity, but kept them for himself. They described his dealing with a bank in Switzerland and collecting American goods in India from his students to resell on the black market, and illegally exchanging money.

They added a fourth reason: affliction with a psychopathic personality. They quote a psychiatric text which defines the incidence of psychopaths to include "unprincipled businessmen, shyster lawyers, quack doctors, high pressure evangelists, crooked politicians to imposters, rapists and prostitutes." In the experience of the authors, Swami Rama falls into several of these categories. He is the high-pressure evangelist in his guise of religious teacher and spiritual guide; he is an unprincipled businessman in his extremely convincing solicitation of funds for 'charity', his dealings in the black market and violations of Indian customs regulations. He is an imposter in his role of 'guru' and in his use of the title "Swami." They go on to describe many different names he'd used in India, and a probable family he had there.

In the second to last paragraph, they included my name and appended my letter to Dr. Green to the document. I admired all their hard work in putting this together. I hoped it would make a difference, but I never expected to hear from the FBI.

It helped that we coalesced into a loosely supportive group. We shared progress and information and since there wasn't a single mirthless person in our group, we shared sarcastic jokes about naive faith. Mimi Wilson put our experiences into cartoons that told the story better than letters or words. Here it was laid out in black and white what we'd been through. Mimi believed us; she knew our broken hearts that dissolved our faith. Over the years I laughed and cried as I revisited these scenes.

The beautiful young devotee is being offered a position to be the head of the institute. I laughed, seeing the bribe that I had refused. Innocently I revealed I was searching for enlightenment, not power and glory. It was the hook Swami Rama used to his advantage with many women.

"Look at these jewels. They belonged to my poor old mother."
Swami loved to give cheap jewelry to his victims. He gave me a Star of
David necklace that was probably given to him by some poor devotee.
When he promised to stop seducing women, he gave me a ring as evi-
dence of his sincerity.

The VISIT

Indriani waited for Swami Rama outside the bank in Switzerland. She was there, she knew it had happened, but we didn't have any written proof, no paper trail.

The 14th's letter

We all got the letter about a meeting on the 14th. It was a time to assure the members that everything was okay, the Meditation Center would continue to do good work, bring discipline.

Waiting in anticipation for the meeting:

Contemplating this big upcoming meeting. Would it clear everything up? But some hoped Arya would see the light and separate the
Meditation Center from Swami Rama's Himalayan Institute.

Someone snuck into the Meditation Center and took the picture of Swami Rama off the wall. I'm sure it was one of the founding members who were with the group before Swami Rama showed up in person. They had dedicated many hours and days to creating this place and wanted it to disassociate from Swami Rama.

Leaving propaganda

Others went to Dinkytown on the University of Minnesota campus and passed out pamphlets that described what Swami Rama had been doing. They left some pamphlets at the Meditation center too. I wished I'd known about the passing out of pamphlets in Dinkytown, I would have driven in from my home an hour away to participate.

The propaganda caused panic at the Meditation Center. There were rumors, and everyone wanted to know: was this the truth?

Truth emerging from the confrence of explanation.

An avalanche of argie-bargie, with quotes out of context from holy texts at the meeting on the 14th, calmed everyone at the Meditation Center. Their eyes closed, and they didn't even have any ears to listen to anything other than what Arya told them. They didn't need to enter into a state of bumfuzzle, and be confused. The truth was that these women simply felt rejected by Swami Rama. They were spreading lies about this poor innocent guru. This let the faithful continue in a state of undisturbed bliss.

The faithfull

After that meeting on the 14th, those who remained at the Meditation Center were full of joyful faith

We were the unfaithful

I felt honored to be included in this group of people dedicated to the truth. I hoped that we could make a difference.

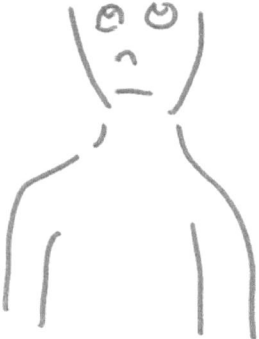

Some of us were described to the faithful as being poor misled inno-
cents. How else could esteemed members of the group like Dan have
believed these lies?

Arya meeting with me and telling me never to come to the Meditation Center again.

Some who were involved were called on the telephone and abruptly excommunicated.

Luckily, they still had their heads and were able to go forth and lead productive lives.

Dr. Arya ordered off the premises people who had worked for the cause for three years.

Excommunication by group. If anyone had the gumption to speak the truth, the faithful members were ordered to make them leave immediately.

We were proud of our rebellion. We laughed and cried as we shared these pictures of ourselves.

CHAPTER 12

Moving Forward
1975-1976

I LOCKED MY CLASSROOM DOOR and breathed a sigh of relief. I liked my job, but I loved the weekend, just being at home, walking the dog, cooking, and cleaning house. Bob and I were saving money and the environment by commuting together. Out in the snow-covered parking lot I waved to my students on the bus, as I proceeded to the highway towards downtown St. Paul. Since it was Friday, he told me to pick him up at the bar he frequented with state employees. I struggled through rush hour traffic and parked on the street. After shoving a couple of coins in the parking meter, I hurried into the bar.

"Bob, let's go," I whispered, not wanting to embarrass him in front of his co-workers. I waited impatiently, I just wanted to get home. He ignored me. "Let's go, the dog is home alone, it has been a long week."

If he didn't care about me, maybe he'd care about the dog.

"Okay, just one more beer." My body started to relax; it had been a long week of teaching middle school kids with learning disabilities. It seemed Bob didn't listen to me at all, as if his ears had earflaps. I tried to be patient, to just love him. But I felt he was still angry at me. It was like the weight, the guilt, of my betrayal, never left. *Could we ever get beyond his anger and my guilt?*

He downed his beer. "Okay, let's go," he growled, and we walked out of the bar to the parking lot.

He slid into the driver's seat without saying a word.

"Maybe I should drive," I suggested, a little late.

"No, I'm fine, I only had about two beers."

I was sure he'd had more than that. It had been three years since he'd gotten his driver's license back. I didn't want to have to drive him everywhere again, or worse yet get killed by his driving while drunk. He started driving down the highway. By the look of his clenched jaw, I knew he wouldn't let me drive. The miles whizzed past at 70 miles per hour. We were out of city and his driving seemed okay. He continued to stare straight ahead while he said through clenched teeth, "You are such a bitch."

I cowered in the passenger seat. *Maybe I am a bitch.* I looked down at the floor mat, wanting to crawl under it. It had been two years since I'd returned from India, but still he didn't trust me.

Suddenly, his hand slapped me across the face.

My face stung, turning red. The stinging jarred me out of my guilt. My heart raced. He'd never hit me. I wasn't going to stay and be beaten up. I slid over against the door as the fields whizzed passed out the window. I reached for the door handle.

No, I can't jump out at this speed, I stiffened my body and pulled my hand away from the door handle. *We can't continue like this*, I gulped and said quietly, "Honey I think we need to get some help. We need to find a marriage counselor if we are ever to get beyond this."

He continued to stare straight ahead, driving on.

"Well, if we're not going to do something about it. Stop this car right now and let me out."

"What?" he asked as if he didn't even realize what he'd just done.

"You just hit me."

"I did?"

He'd had more the two beers for sure. I stopped the conversation until the next morning, and then he agreed to go to a marriage counselor.

I made some phone calls and found a marriage counselor named Dottie. Our health insurance covered the cost. Dottie was young, not much older than we were. She had short curly black hair that stopped above her shoulders, and an infectious smile. She attacked the obvious problem head on.

"Do you understand how much you hurt Bob?" she asked.

I just looked at the floor, a sense of guilt and shame overwhelmed me. I wanted to cry but tears wouldn't come. I was unable to speak, *Did I understand?* Finally, my mouth opened, "I don't know, I don't know anything any more." My heart felt heavy, my chest did not want to rise and fall because of the weight.

I turned towards him, looking down, still unable to look at him. A scene flashed through my mind of the phone call from Jeremy where he predicted that I would hurt this young boy who'd never been hurt. Slowly I put my head up looking at him and blurted out, "I am so sorry that I hurt you. I was a stupid idiot."

He seemed to soften before my eyes. He wasn't perfect, I wasn't perfect, but still, we could love one another.

He said, "I'm sorry I hit you."

"I believe you."

"It won't happen again," he said.

Dottie knew that I was unhappy. I complained about doing all the housework. She said, "Well, just don't do it all." She assigned us homework. "Write each other a letter about what you do each day, and what you do together."

I still have that paper. As I read it, looking back, I can't believe everything that I did. I went to work, paid all the bills, did all the housework, and all the cooking. I was still trying to be superwoman, just like in high school, only now I was a grown woman. I wrote *I totally failed at not doing things. When they piled up, I just did them... I asked you to help me consistently and you said you would help when you want to, and I could shove it up my ass.*

Bob acknowledged I did the housework. He said, *"My mother always did all of the housework, but then she didn't work outside the home too. Maybe I could do the vacuuming."*

From then on, he vacuumed. He kept the cars running and shoveled snow.

Over that six months of weekly counseling, Dottie did more than just work on the relationship between the two of us. She also looked at the problems we brought with us to the marriage. She had Bob act out how he'd felt with his father. I'd met his parents, but he'd never said much about his childhood. Dottie said, "Here, let's role play. I'm your dad. How would you approach me?"

I watched with my mouth open as Bob got down on the floor and practically crawled towards his father, afraid of him.

We'd only visited his parents in the politest situations. I didn't know that his father had gotten drunk almost every weekend. I'd never seen his father like that.

She had me come in alone and asked me about my family. I still really didn't want to talk about it. I talked about the stranger that tried to rape me, but I was so ashamed of the situation that happened with my brother I hesitated to mention it. Dottie sensed that I was leaving something out. "What else happened?" she asked looking me squarely in the eyes.

"Well, my older brother used to sneak into my room and touch me. I never told anyone about this except my mother, not even Bob."

"You know that's sexual abuse too, don't you?"

I blinked my eyes, "What?" I blurted out. "He was my brother. He didn't get on top of me, he didn't really rape me. Mother said it was my fault."

"How could it be your fault? You were four years younger."

I just sank down in my chair. Somehow, I'd never thought about it as abuse.

"This is your brother. Maybe you should call him up and ask him to apologize."

"I have to see him every holiday, when he comes home. He lives far away. He gives me nice presents at Christmas. Other than that, we don't talk."

"Call. What have you got to lose?" she said.

It seemed like a good idea, "Okay, I'll call him."

I kept putting the phone call off. I'd pick up the telephone receiver and then, put it back down, afraid. I really didn't know what Dennis would say. What if he got mad at me? I could lose the unspeaking peace that existed on holidays, yet I hoped he would apologize. Maybe we could laugh about our childhood and finally be friends.

Finally, I dialed his number. Slowly the numbers curled around the dial and came back. I hesitated; my heart thumped loudly as I heard the long-distance ring. I wanted to hang it up. But then I heard, "Hello," his deep voice reverberated in the phone.

"Hello, this is your sister," I said.

"I know that, of course you're my sister, I only have one, nit wit."

There it was again, an insult, I hesitated, but still I blundered onwards. I jumped right into the question, "Huh, do you remember saying that maybe I'd need counseling one day?"

"No, I never said that," he answered.

'But... but I remember you did say that.' I swallowed hard. "I'm in counseling now. And... and I'd like you to apologize for what you did to me."

"I'm in a totally different place now. I don't see why I should apologize," he answered.

I took a deep breath, holding back tears. I wanted to throw the phone at him. Instead, I just hung up and sat there, shaking. The anger seethed all through my body; my stomach turned itself in knots. *Why couldn't he just apologize, just an "I'm sorry" would help so much.* I buried my head in my hands.

At the next appointment, I told Dottie all about it. Her young soft brown eyes looked at me and saw my pain. "I'm so sorry," she said.

I also talked to her about Bob's drinking. "Instead of coming home, Bob goes to the bar, and I never know when he'll get home."

"We'll talk about that at your next session together."

The next session she sat upright at her desk and surprised me. She said, "Why don't you stop drinking for a month?

Bob said, "Sure, I don't have a problem drinking. This will prove it."

My spirits rose to new heights when he agreed. I'd never expected him to ever quit drinking.

Bob didn't drink for a month but that whole time he seemed on edge. It was like he was gritting his teeth. He seemed like he was very nervous, sometimes his hand would shake when he held it out.

After his month of tense sobriety Bob started to drink again. He said it was because he hated his job. He quit his research job and went to technical school to become a building maintenance engineer. I hoped that would help him stop drinking but instead, he came home from class and went back to the bar every afternoon. He could easily drink and manage the assignments.

I'd stopped using birth control two years earlier. My biological clock was ticking, and my body longed to hold a baby. This was the new age of family planning - we were supposed to be able to plan a family. I thought, once I stopped using birth control, I'd get pregnant right away. We tried and tried, but nothing had happened. We even hung a fertility doll above the waterbed. It didn't help.

Two months later we went on a motorcycle trip, and I had an awful backache. I went to the doctor and was shocked when he said, "You're three months pregnant." I hadn't been paying attention to my periods. The conception occurred during the month Bob had stopped drinking.

I was terrified. I just hadn't expected this. I was just starting a new job. I had to walk in and tell the principal who'd just hired me that I was pregnant. He was matter of fact and said, "You will need to go on leave a month before the baby is due."

After that I went up to my shared classroom and approached my new co-worker, Helen Johnson. Together we made up the special education department for North Branch Middle School. Helen was an older experienced teacher with grown children. I tried to keep tears from running down my cheeks as I blurted out, "I'm sorry, but I'm pregnant."

She walked up to me and gave me a big hug. "That's wonderful," she said.

All of my fears evaporated. I worked as long as I could at my teaching job. My teaching contract demanded that I take unpaid maternity leave a month before my due date. I sat at home and stared at the empty crib full of presents from my baby shower. *Was I ever going to have a baby to hold in my arms?* My belly got bigger and bigger. I hobbled out to the mailbox thinking this must be what it's like to be old. I was desperate, as I only had a three-month leave from my job, and Bob wasn't working. He spent as much time as he could at the bar.

Finally, when I was a month overdue, I went in to the hospital to be induced on the day before my own birthday. I asked for it to be the day before because I didn't want to share my special St. Patrick's Day birthday. They started the drip, a doctor stopped by and said, "It's a boy." I started contractions, but still hardly any dilation. Hours went by, still nothing. Around midnight March 16, 1976, the doctor called for a team to come and do an emergency C-section.

The doctors discovered they didn't have my O negative blood on hand in this small-town hospital. I felt the cold table under my body, my legs in stirrup. Every five minutes I had a contraction, but nothing happened. After an hour the blood had arrived from the city and the anesthesiologist said, "Everything will be okay," as I finally fell asleep.

My family waited outside the door, not sure if I was alive or dead - nobody came out to talk to them about the wait for my blood type. Finally, after two hours, at a minute after midnight on my birthday, March 17th, they handed me a large baby girl with long straight black hair and blue almond-shaped eyes.

When Bob was allowed in to look at the baby, he shook his head, not sure where the black hair came from. He almost acted like he thought it wasn't his baby. My mother looked and said, "Maybe she's a throwback to my mother; she had long dark hair." I was too drugged to care. But I knew it was his baby, there hadn't been anyone else.

When Bob's parents arrived, they smiled at the baby and had no problem with her black hair. "Bob was born with black hair too. It will fall out and come in blond." they said. "Most Finnish babies are born with black hair."

I'd forgotten I had married a Finn. Bob had spoken only Finnish until he was five years old.

They wheeled me into my recovery room that was shared with a mom who'd just had a normal delivery. She was sitting up in bed smoking a cigarette and talking loudly on the telephone.

I felt nauseated from the anesthesia and the cigarette smoke. I crawled into the bathroom and lay on the floor away from the cigarette smoke. Finally, the nurse found me there and got me a room of my own.

The nurse wheeled baby Alice into my room and asked, "Do you need help?" as she gently placed her in my arms.

"No," I said, and the nurse left the room. I'd read all the books I could find about nursing. I was sure this was natural, so it should be easy.

I sat up in bed with a pillow covering the stitches which stretched from my belly button down to my shaved pubic hairs. I held Alice with both arms up to my bulging breasts. Instead of latching on, Alice turned her head away.

Oh no, I don't know how to do this, my heart started to race. *Stupid, stupid, I should have asked for help.*

Still, I didn't press the call button, I didn't want to admit my stupidity. I brought up the image of a picture from the book I'd read and tried to replicate the instructions. With Alice's head balanced in my right elbow. Using my left hand, I picked up my heavy right breast overflowing with milk and shoved it into Alice's little mouth. She latched on, and I relaxed. *This is what those breasts are for.* A feeling of joy filled my entire being.

CHAPTER 13

The New Baby and a Visit from the FBI

1976

THE HOSPITAL BILLS WERE piling up and I had no idea how we would ever pay them. With the surgery we'd gone way over the $600 limit my health insurance had on maternity bills. I was very weak but insisted on going home as soon as possible.

They'd cut my intestines during the surgery and insisted that I pass gas before they'd allow me to go home. I tossed and turned, my stomach - bloated with gas - finally exploded out through the proper channels. Two days after the surgery I was allowed to leave the hospital.

The nurse wheeled me out of my room and helped me into the car. She handed me baby Alice. I looked down at her, sleeping peacefully in my arms, truly the best birthday present ever. But her head was facing towards the door of the car. I worried, *What if we had a car accident on the way home?*

I told Bob, "Stop the car, I need to hold her the other way around, Mom told me not to carry her this way. If we got side-swiped, that would be the end of her."

He stopped the car and opened the passenger door, gently turning her around so her soft head was away from the door. It was a thirty-minute drive on a narrow-paved road through Avery Game Reserve to our home on Coon Lake Beach. I hardly noticed the sunshine glistening on the snow-covered pine trees on either side of the road. Every bump made me clench my jaw to try to stop from yelling out in pain. The stitches in my abdomen were red and raw, yelling at me to lie down in bed.

After thirty minutes we arrived home safely. Bob carried Alice in and carefully placed her in a bassinet someone had given us. I was too weak to carry her. I sank down into the waterbed, totally exhausted. As soon as he'd gotten me in the bed, Bob said, "I'm going out to the bar for a little while."

The Ramblers was only three blocks away. As I drifted off to sleep, I heard the door click shut. I thought, *He'll be back soon,* smiling to myself.

I woke up to the baby crying and no one else in the house. I tried to get up, but with my stomach muscles cut open from the C-section, I couldn't move. The water sloshed underneath me as I struggled to get up. "Bob, Bob, help," I called out, but no one answered.

I closed my eyes and clenched my teeth, muttering, *How can he do this?* All while the screams of our hungry baby reverberated in my ears. I turned on my side and grabbed the board on the edge of the bed. Slowly I pulled myself up and wobbled towards the bassinet holding onto furniture along the way. Every step felt like my abdomen was on fire.

Finally, I reached the bassinet and stared down in the squeezed together eyes of my screaming red-faced baby. Thoughts panicked through my mind. *I'm not even sure I know how to pick her up correctly. What if I don't support her head right?* In the hospital, they'd just handed her to me, I hadn't picked her up by myself. She was a newborn.

Pushing my stomach against the bassinet to brace my cut muscles, I leaned over and picked her up, supporting her head, placing her on my shoulder. She stopped crying while I sat down next to the phone and dialed my mother. Mother was in Minneapolis, an hour's drive away. With each number I dialed with my finger, my mind called out, *Help*. The phone rang and my voice whispered, "Can you please come out here and help? I don't know what to do. The baby's crying and Bob's gone to the bar."

"He did what?" she asked, almost yelling.

"He... he went to the bar," I said, ashamed to admit my husband would do such a thing. "I don't know when he'll be back."

"Don't worry, I'll be there as soon as I can."

Tears filled my eyes as I sat down in a rocking chair and held Alice to my breast. She grabbed on and suckled. The pain in my abdomen subsided, and I relaxed. *Mother will be here in an hour*, I thought, as tears flowed down my face, knowing Bob was still at the bar.

Alice and I were still alone in the rocking chair an hour later, when Mother burst through the kitchen door, suitcase in hand. Tears of relief filled my eyes. She said she'd stay overnight and sleep on the couch. But she stayed not just one night, but for an entire week. I was never again as close to my mother as I was during that week. She brought not just knowledge, but love, caring and history. She showed me how to bathe the baby and to swaddle her in a receiving blanket, so she'd feel safe. She brought history in lovely cotton receiving blankets she had saved from when I was a baby.

Bob kept his distance from the baby, as if he was afraid of this tiny creature. He refused to touch a diaper, sure that if he did, he would vomit.

Slowly I got better, I felt confident to be on my own by the time Mother left. My face glowed with joy as I sat in the rocking chair, rocking my baby girl for hours, she and I encircled in a cocoon of motherly love. The snow melted and spring green started to show on the trees. Soon I'd have to leave her and go back to work. I'd only been home with Alice for three weeks, but I'd spent too much of that time just sitting worrying that we were broke.

Bob sold his guitar because we hardly had money for food. He went to classes and the bar; I rarely saw him.

One day, while I was home alone rocking the baby, there was a knock at the door. I got up to answer it, holding Alice over my shoulder. I opened the door and was shocked to see two large men on my doorstep.

"Hello, are you Pat Stierna?" they asked in unison.

I stood staring at them; and reached to slam the door shut in their faces. I was scared. I didn't have any idea why two strange men in business suits, would show up at my door when I was home alone.

"Sorry to disturb you ma'am, but we're from the FBI," the short stocky man on the left said quickly, before I shut the door. He pulled a leather holder out of his pocket and flashed his ID at me. The tall thin man on the right did the same. The thin guy said, "We're looking for Pat Stierna to answer some questions."

"I'm Pat Stierna," I answered, not sure what this was about.

"We're investigating someone named Swami Rama, and we heard you were willing to testify."

"Oh, okay. Come in," I said, letting out an almost audible sigh of relief. I told my friends I'd testify, but I was surprised that the FBI hadn't called first.

"You sure have a beautiful place out here, but hard to find. We spent two days looking for it."

I thought, *Why didn't they just call me. My number's in the phone book. I could have told you how to get here.*

"I'll get you some coffee," I said, which is the standard response of any civil Minnesotan, when a visitor stops by. I went into the kitchen and put the coffee pot on. Then I came back and sat down on the couch facing them. *Finally, there was a real investigation of Swami Rama,* I thought.

"Do you know Swami Rama?" the short guy asked, while the skinny guy wrote everything down in a notebook with a slick-looking ballpoint pen.

"Yes, I was introduced to him by Dr. Arya who had been my Sanskrit teacher at the University of Minnesota."

"Did you have some sort of encounter with Swami Rama?" the skinny guy asked.

"Yes, I did, but it wasn't as bad as what happened to the other women, probably because I was married," I said as I got up, turning my back on them. I took a deep breath, trying to keep from shaking as I poured them their cups of coffee.

I didn't really want to tell these guys my story, but if it would get Swami Rama out of the country, and get him to stop what he was doing, I'd tell everything I'd experienced.

First, I told what I'd learned from other people. "Did you see the letter from Tom about how he had purchased LSD for him? We think he used it to initiate people. They also think he has been smuggling things. Plus, he took girls to India and used them sexually."

"Yes, we heard of these things, but what was your direct experience?" asked the short stocky guy.

I started to tell them the story of how I'd been seduced. They seemed way too interested, their eyes gleamed at me, and I detected a smirk in the corners of their mouths.

"I went to the Menninger Foundation to do research on my thesis, and while I was there, I went to hear a lecture by Swami Rama. I had been told that Swami Rama was celibate, so I wasn't concerned when he asked me to stay for some special instruction."

"Did he forcibly rape you?"

No, he did not, but he seduced me under false pretenses."

"Oh, interesting. And how did he do that?" the agent taking notes said, perking up.

"Well, he told me I was his wife from a previous life, and I believed him," I said, feeling like an utter idiot.

They got up to leave, but as they went out the door, the skinny guy turned around and said, "There's just one thing I'd like to know."

"What's that?" I asked innocently.

"We'd just like to know HOW he did that," he said, laughing, and slapping his partner on the arm.

I felt horrified. They just thought it was funny. I felt violated. As if he'd wanted to seduce me too.

After they left, I collapsed onto the couch, holding my baby girl in my arms. Don't they understand at all? He violated the essence of my spiritual beliefs. He filled my meditations with fear. To this day I'm afraid to meditate like I did before. I know it's nonsense, but I feared he could come into my mind, and control me.

I put Alice in her bassinet, and she fell asleep. Then I collapsed onto the waterbed. I was so relieved to have those awful men out of my house. I fell into a deep sleep as the water in the bed rose and fell with each breath. I didn't need any men.

The next day I called Debbie, "I was so excited the FBI came, I thought they'd take me seriously, but then when they left, they just smirked at me. They wanted to know how they could do it too."

"Hopefully they listened to the guys. They met with them at Bridgeman's last week."

"Bridgeman's, really? The ice cream parlor? I don't know, they seemed more interested in how, than in what, Swami Rama did."

Although Alice was just four weeks old, I had to go back to work. We needed money desperately. The school counselor lived across the street from the school, and I hired his wife to babysit. At lunch time I raced over to nurse, my breasts dripping with milk. Alice latched on while I nibbled my sandwich, overjoyed to be back with my little girl.

Each morning I got Alice and myself off to work. When I got home, Bob was either at the bar or in the basement, drinking. One evening after work I walked down into the basement workshop and saw him sitting there on piled up cardboard cases of Budweiser bottles at the work bench. More boxes were piled against the walls, he was drinking almost a case of beer a day. My nose wrinkled as I inhaled the stale smell of it. He'd always said since he just drank beer, he couldn't be an alcoholic like his dad, who drank hard liquor. His hand shook as he lifted the bottle to his lips and sucked his Budweiser. I turned my back to the sight and raced up the stairs. Where was my husband, my helpmate, a father for our baby?

The school year was ending soon, and I didn't feel well. I took Excedrin and kept going, just a couple more days and the school year would be over.

Bob came home and wobbled over to me. "Let me hold the baby," he said.

"Okay." I said, surprised he wanted to help. I walked over to him and stopped. The smell of stale beer filled my nostrils. His hair was plastered to his head, like he hadn't had a bath in weeks. I'd been so busy caring for the baby and going to work I hadn't noticed. I handed the baby over, and she immediately started crying.

"Why is she crying?" he asked.

"Maybe she doesn't like the smell of beer," I answered. My insult didn't even register with Bob, his eyes glazed with alcohol. I watched him holding Alice, anger arose in me, *I don't have one child, I have two.*

The baby continued to cry.

"She doesn't like me," he whined. His hands shook as he handed her back to me.

I took her back in my arms and she immediately stopped crying.

"She doesn't know you. You can't even hold her without shaking." I stared at him and saw him for the drunk he had become. I decided. I was going to file for a divorce, but I didn't say anything, stroking Alice's fragile head.

CHAPTER 14

Illness
1976

THOSE CRIES WERE a call for help. She didn't want to have a drunk father. I didn't have to live with a drunk. I had a baby to care for. I didn't need two children, one who should be a father.

Bob was working part time. I never knew when he might walk in on me, so I used a friend's phone. I called a women's organization to find a female lawyer. I didn't want to deal with any men. After that interview with the FBI, I didn't even want to talk to another man. That had been weeks ago, but the terror of having been looked at as a sex object was still fresh in my memory. As I dialed the phone, my hand shook. I made the appointment and noted to remember to bring my checkbook and a statement of my income, and Bob's income, which was nothing at the time.

It was my last week of teaching before summer vacation. I left work early and showed up at the lawyer's house, with a check for $100, and our financial papers. Her office was in her home. A skinny looking young man wandered around the backyard looking like he was stoned. She saw me staring at him and explained that it was her son who was moving out soon. "It's difficult to raise a child alone," she said, with a sad, knowing look on her face.

Financially things looked good... I had a good job, and since I had made most of the house payments, the house would be mine. When she said, "Since he is the father of your child, he must be allowed to visit her." I was horrified. More than anything else I wanted to keep my baby away from him. I didn't want to hear that cry anymore—the frantic cry she made when he held her in his shaking arms. I wanted to pull her back into my arms and protect her from even the smell of him.

I left the lawyer's office, exhausted. My head ached and strange red bumps covered my legs. I'd been swallowing aspirin to keep going just one more week. I had to work. I was bringing in the only consistent income. I thought the headache was tension and the bumps a rash.

The school year was over, and I was finally able to be at home with my baby. But when I tried to get out of bed, I couldn't. My arms felt like lead weights and refused to respond when I tried to lift them. *How was I going to take care of the baby?* It took both arms to lift my hand to my forehead. It was sticky with perspiration. I reached for the Excedrin I'd been taking for two weeks straight. I fumbled with the bottle, even my fingers would not move properly. As I collapsed back into bed. Alice started to cry.

I struggled and managed to get up out of bed. My legs worked, but they were covered with red bumps, like mosquito bites, but I hadn't been anywhere to have gotten bitten. I walked to the bassinet; each step felt like I was lifting ten tons. I stood over the crib and stared down at Alice. Her little mouth was open, screaming. She was such a helpless little thing. Slowly I managed to lean over and jerkily lift her to my shoulder. We collapsed together into the rocking chair. She suckled my hot sticky breast, and I tried to think what to do.

I stumbled over to the telephone and dialed Sharon, my neighbor. "I'm sick, I have to go to the doctor. Could you watch the baby for me?"

My neighborhood, Coon Lake Beach, was like a little town. Even people I'd hardly known had brought me presents when Alice was born. Sharon came over immediately.

Each movement as I reached down and pulled on my pants to dress was like lifting weights. *What was wrong with me?*

I drove through the woods to Forest Lake, the closest town, thirty minutes away. I was relieved that Dr. Olson was in the clinic that day. He'd been there when Alice was born. I trusted him. The nurse took my temperature. Even with the Excedrin it was 101. He took one look at me, holding my legs, mussing over the red bumps.

"This is definitely *Erythema nodosum*," he said. "Have you had strep throat recently? "

"No, I don't think so. I had a headache, but I just took aspirin and kept working. I had to finish the school year," I said, confused. My mind yelled, *What is he talking about?*

"This is a very serious illness. It is a complication from a strep infection and requires complete bedrest," he said.

I sat there staring at him, as my body started to shake. "I can't be sick, I have a tiny baby to care for," I said, out loud this time.

"Do you have anyone you can stay with?" he asked gently. I hadn't told him, that my husband was useless, but somehow, he knew.

I used the clinic phone and called my mother. The doctor didn't want me to leave without a plan in place.

"Mom," I said tears welling up in my eyes. "I'm sick. Dr. Olson says I need complete bed rest. Could you come and pick up the baby and me?"

I managed to drive myself home. Mother was already there when I arrived. As soon as I saw her the words just tumbled out of my mouth, "I met with a lawyer, and she's going to file divorce papers for me. Bob is just drunk all the time."

Mom didn't look at me; she just looked towards the ground, and I saw tears pool in the corner of her eye. I remembered Mom had separated from her first husband. For her, this must just be like history repeating itself. As soon as I got inside the house I fell back into bed and Mother did everything.

She loaded her car with diapers, Alice's clothes, and some clothes for me. I struggled to sit up and grabbed a pen and paper. My hand shook as I wrote, "I'm sick. I'm going to Mom's. She is going to take care of the baby and me." I didn't mention the divorce, the lawyer said she'd call him about that.

When we arrived at my childhood home, Mother made a bed for me on the couch. It was the same room I'd shared as a child with my younger brother, Eugene. Mom had squeezed three beds in there after my father died. But the room was now back functioning as a living room. The same large mirror sat above the fireplace. I stared into it seeing the face of an unrecognizable exhausted woman. My hair hung in limp strings down the sides of my face. I sunk down on the couch and Mother covered me with a blanket.

Mother changed Alice's diapers and cared for her. She only brought her in for me to nurse, other than that I slept on the couch, snuggling protected in a warm cocoon. Years later, after she died, I found a letter she'd written to her sister, describing that time. She wrote, "It all made me so sad. At times I was at my wits' end."

The next day the lawyer called Bob and explained that I had filed for a divorce. Bob called me at Mom's and said quietly, "I just want to ask you one thing. Do you love me?"

He didn't ask how I was feeling, he didn't believe I was sick.

"Not any more," I answered, feeling the red spots on my legs heat up at the sound of his voice

He started to cry and carry on about how he couldn't live without me. It was an old story, but this time I knew I couldn't live with him. If my mind couldn't tell me, my body had.

Every time I saw him or even talked to him; the inflammation got worse. He kept stumbling into Mom's house to see the baby. Mom kept him in the other room away from me. But I still heard Alice crying when he held her. I wished I was strong enough to go and snatch her away from him.

A week later he called, demanding that Mother let him talk to me. Reluctantly she handed me the phone, "I called Dottie, our counselor" he said. "Dottie suggested I go to St. Mary's Treatment Center. I'll quit drinking just like you always wanted."

"That's nice," I answered, "But I don't care any more." He started to sob again. I hung up. I couldn't stand it. I had to get well.

Maybe Dottie's suggestion would help him. I'd had enough. I'd rather not see him ever again.

The day of his appointment at St. Mary's, Bob stopped at Mom's house, so drunk he could hardly walk. He said, "I'm gonna slop drinking just like you always wanted," his words slurring together. They're gonna tell me if I need inpatient or outpatient over at the hospital."

I stood in the doorway to the living room and stared at him. All I wanted was for him to stay away from me. He was driving our car when he couldn't walk a straight line. I prayed he wouldn't kill somebody before he arrived at the hospital.

An hour later he called from the hospital. He said someone was going home with him to get his clothes. He was going to stay at the hospital as an inpatient. A wave of relief swept through me as I realized he wouldn't be stumbling over to Mom's asking to see me and the baby.

The day after, a woman from the hospital called and wanted to speak to me. I felt a tremor of cold fear go through me as I spoke to her. "Yes, he is my husband, but I don't want anything to do with him. We are getting a divorce."

"Okay", she answered, "But you still need to come over to the hospital. He needs your help and input for him to get well. The program is for you too. Did you know that eight out of ten spouses of alcoholics end up remarrying alcoholics?"

"No, I didn't know that," I replied. The thought of it terrified me. "I'll come in tomorrow." I said, wanting to get this over with as soon as possible.

The next day, still weak from my illness, I drove across the Mississippi River to St. Mary's Hospital and found a parking spot inside the ramp. I stepped gingerly from the car and walked slowly through the hall, taking in the clean sterile hospital smell. My teeth were clenched as I turned the knob on the counselor's door.

A friendly woman offered me a seat. Just the two of us sat in a tiny room. She wasn't even behind a desk, just in a chair seated beside me. I let my guard down and the tears flowed. I cried the entire time we talked. I agreed to make a list of incidents where Bob's drinking had hurt me, and to come to Family Day the next Tuesday.

Sunday Bob talked me into coming to see him. He looked clean and neat. I sat down on the edge of the bed, keeping my distance. When he moved closer, I moved away. He was enthusiastic, showing me piles of books he had read.

He said, "I'm taking a bath every day. One of the symptoms of alcoholism is not taking care of yourself."

I stayed on the far edge of the bed. He certainly looked better and smelled better too, but I wasn't getting any closer.

His eyes had the sad look of a pathetic little puppy begging to be forgiven. I kept my cool distance. But I took the book *I'll Quit Tomorrow* by Vernon E. Johnson, back to Mom's, agreeing to read it. I had no idea what an eye opener that book would be.

CHAPTER 15

Treatment
1976-1978

THAT VERY EVENING, I started reading *I'll Quit Tomorrow*. The introduction detailed the disease of alcoholism, now classified as alcohol-use disorder, or alcohol dependence. On page one Bob underlined:

"The most significant characteristics of the disease are that it is primary, progressive, chronic, and fatal. But it can be arrested."

A disease? Is it really a disease? I thought he was just being an asshole, so cock sure of himself, always right, never helping around the house.

Page two stated that three out of four of St. Mary's patients successfully recover from alcoholism and Bob underlined:

"You find that this disease is an entity as distinct as measles. Alcoholism has a describable, predictable pattern of pathology. It is primary in the sense that it effectively blocks any care or treatment we might want to deliver to any other problem..." The alcoholic "is a formidable person to confront, and it is true he is able skillfully to rationalize his own behavior. He is loaded with self-hatred which is repressed and unconscious and he projects this onto persons around him." (P. 4)

That's why he always had an answer. It was always my fault; everything was my fault.

I took out my pencil - if he could write in the book, then I'd write in it, too. He'd underlined:

"The people around an alcoholic do not realize how little he knows of himself and of his own behavior. He is not confronted by his own actions; many of them he is not even aware of, although those around him assume he is."

Does this mean he wasn't even aware of leaving me at home ill with a new baby? I was surprised, as he was always so together, always blaming me, so of course I thought he knew what he was doing. I wrote in the margin, "Yes, I was one of those people"

The book described the progression of alcoholism and Bob described in the margin how he himself went through the steps which started in 1964 before I met him, and with binge drinking. Plus, he had the example and genetics of his alcoholic father. First, he became a happy social drinker, developing a relationship with alcohol and it lifted his mood every time. At some point for the alcoholic this happy social relationship becomes a preoccupation with getting the next drink. The alcoholic becomes uncomfortable when not drinking.

"If a person is alcoholic, by definition he is unable to recognize the fact. Any attempt to interrupt his drinking or change his lifestyle he views as meddling. Every time you rescue an alcoholic you are delaying his treatment." (P. 59)

I listed in the margin the times I'd rescued him, starting back in college when:

1. I'd paid him 25 cents an hour for studying. He'd said he didn't have time to study because he had to have a job to buy cigarettes and beer.

2. We moved out of town, a geographic cure.

3. I started to pay all the bills.

4. I let him quit his job and start graduate school. He told me his job made him drink.

5. He dropped out of graduate school and went to trade school.

6. I worked all the time.

7. I worked on the house, cleaned the gutters, painted over the peeling paint, changed the storm windows, and raked the leaves all by myself.

In all caps I wrote: I'M NOT GOING TO DO ANY OF IT ANY MORE.

The book had me hooked. I stayed up all night, reading. It read like the story of our marriage. My defense hackles started to rise when I read the chapter on Rational Defenses and Projection. It described the alcoholic family, especially the spouse.

"The only difference between the alcoholic and the spouse, in instances where the latter does not drink, is that one is physically affected by alcohol; otherwise, both have all the other symptoms. The dry is as sick as the drunk, except that the bodily damage is not there. With every drunk there is a sick dry; it's almost a mirror image." (P. 30).

Bob had even double-underlined this. It goes on to claim that the spouse would say, "I don't need help. It's his problem, not mine."

I wrote, "I haven't done those things since we worked with the counselor Dottie, and I did get help." I'd been cured; *I don't need help anymore, fuck 'em all,* I thought, with all my defenses on high alert.

All that toughness began to soften when I read what Bob wrote at the end of the book that gave me hope. He wrote:

Pat,
The love of a sick man is perverted. As I return to health, the true love that was buried so long is once again beginning to blossom.

Holding these words cautiously in my subconscious, I was able to go to Family Day the following Tuesday. Terrible Tuesday is what the people in treatment called it. It was definitely not a happy party time.

Mom watched Alice while I drove over to St. Mary's, which was just across the river from Mom's home. I found the room and sat down with an empty chair next to me. Bob came in and sat in a chair right next to mine, his eyes gleaming like we were on a date. I tried to move my chair away from him. I felt my shoulders tense immediately; they only started to relax when the counselors sent the alcoholics out of the room to go to their own groups.

Left in that room with me were twenty-five other concerned persons, seated in rows on hard folding chairs. Mothers, wives, husbands, fathers, brothers, sisters, adult children, and lovers - people whose loved ones suffered from the disease of alcoholism. We had all lived with that disease and therefore, we too were sick, or so the counselor told us. That was a lot to swallow. How could I be sick in the head? I was recovering from *Erythema nodosum*, a physical illness. I was the one who kept everything going; the one who paid the bills, fed the family, changed the flat tire, and got the car repaired.

The group leader, a tough no-nonsense woman with short dark hair stood at the podium in the front and asked, "Why did you stick around and do all that? What was your motivation? What was your reward for doing everything?"

Never one to keep my mouth shut, even in a lecture, I answered, "I did it because I thought I loved him. I'd married him."

"But you helped the alcoholic drink, just by keeping things going," the counselor stated.

"Well, what was I to do, starve to death?" almost spitting the words out through gritted teeth.

If I had been egotistical, I might have walked out right then, but I was too curious, too tired, and too scared to leave. I did not want to marry another alcoholic.

"You stayed with your husband because you are a martyr, a controller, or maybe afraid of change," the counselor said.

As more was said, I reluctantly found myself in their definitions. I had been the martyr who stayed with him through thick and thin. After all, he had said he couldn't live without me. The neighbors told me what a wonderful person I was to stay with him. I controlled the money. I changed jobs, so I could pick Bob up on my way home from work. That way he couldn't get another DWI.

I was reluctant to change. I had dreamed of leaving him many times, my only excuse for staying was my dog. Now I had a baby, and after nine years of marriage, the baby had forced a change in my life.

After the lecture we met in small groups, sitting in a circle with the alcoholics. Each person sat across from their alcoholic, not next to them. Seated this way, they could talk directly to their alcoholic. I listened, clutching my list of things he had done. I twisted the list around my fingers, while I listened to other people read their lists. Many of the alcoholics had done worse things, beaten their wives, run around with other women, smashed up cars, etc. But that didn't make me feel any less angry. I wanted to hurt him like he had hurt me.

"I came home from the hospital, too sick to get out of bed, but you left me with a newborn infant and went to the bar," I said, glaring at him on the other side of the room. I watched him cringe as I said it, loving every minute. I wanted to take a dagger out and thrust it into his stomach, and then turn it so he could feel how my stomach felt whenever that drunk husband came close to me.

The counselor read the anger in my voice and said, "Revenge is not the purpose of this program. Your list will give him some data to work with; things he did while under the influence that he may not have remembered."

I backed off a little. If this was actually an illness, I did want him to get well. But I felt better after venting my anger. It would be a long time before that anger would dissipate, and I could let it go.

This treatment program was paid for by my school health insurance. Bob was an inpatient for five weeks and then there was a two-year follow up program called Growth Group, that met once a week.

I did not pursue the divorce, but I couldn't live with Bob either. Every time I thought about the divorce, I saw the image of that strange young man in the lawyer's backyard, and her excuse saying, "It's hard to raise a child alone". I didn't want to raise a child alone. I went home and back to work; he went to live with John, a long-time friend of ours from college. We'd looked at group homes, for continued treatment after the five weeks in the hospital, but they were too expensive.

In September, when I started teaching again, I found it just too much – teaching, picking Alice up from the babysitter and then going home with her to an empty house. Bob stayed with John for two months, keeping sober and attending AA meetings. My heart melted when I watched him hold Alice, and now that he didn't smell like stale beer or shake when he held her, she smiled up at him. Her black hair had already fallen out, and wisps of blond hair mirrored that of her father's. Every Wednesday we dropped Alice off with my mother and went to Growth Group together. I took a chance and asked him to move back home. I was willing to try again.

To my surprise Bob really helped. He was different. He managed to get a job working as a building maintenance engineer for an insurance company. Instead of going to the bar to drink, he'd come home from work, and actually be there at dinner time. After dinner he'd run off to an AA meeting. When he left, I'd have a sinking feeling in my gut, sure that he'd come back drunk. But instead, he'd return home after two hours with a smile on his face. He even smelled like the young man I'd married.

I still didn't feel free to talk to him at home about his behaviors or my feelings. In the past I had allowed him to convince me that my feelings were silly, not based on fact, and therefore irrelevant. In Growth Group I felt validated, learned that my feelings were facts, no matter how silly Bob might say they were.

Early in our marriage Bob had drawn a picture of a monster that was hidden just behind a fence, that he said was his feelings. The monster had huge claws that hung over the fence - the eyes just barely peeping over a wooden barricade like the walls of a fort. In Growth Group he learned that he too had feelings, good, bad, angry, sad, but they were feelings, not angry monsters to be hidden. This all happened in the fall of 1976.

Falling back in love was a slow process, that happened in Growth Group as he learned to express his feelings and I learned to honor mine. Love is trust and we were rebuilding trust from the bottom up.

In 1977, we were still going to Growth Group once a week. I'd really enjoyed the summer at home with my baby. Bob had managed to get a professional job doing market research for Continental Telephone. Back at work in the fall, I was in full swing, as a working super mom. I made two pumpkin pies for my home room group at the Middle School and put them in the back seat of our new Honda Civic. Our finances had straightened out and we bought a new car. It was the last day before the four-day Thanksgiving vacation. I was even ready for Christmas. I'd already bought and wrapped our Christmas presents.

I dropped Alice off at a local babysitter. As I drove through the woods towards work, gentle snow was falling, covering everything except a single track in the middle of the road. I drove slowly and carefully, when suddenly a large car appeared in my path. I turned the steering wheel towards the ditch, pushing on the accelerator. The wheels spun in the icy snow rut, and the car didn't turn. The little Honda Civic continued on straight on towards this larger older car. The world went black.

When I woke up, I was sitting in a crushed car, with a big hole in my knee, and I was freezing. A neighbor had seen the accident and brought out a blanket. "The ambulance is on the way," he said. I didn't think of anything, except I knew I was going to be late for work. The medic arrived and cut me out of the car, carefully putting me on a stretcher.

"What day is it?" the medic asked.

I didn't know what day it was, only that I needed to be at work. I answered, "Please call North Branch Middle School and tell them I'm going to be late," of course, there wasn't a phone in the ambulance. I heard a distant siren roaring and realized it was the thing I was riding in. We skidded through an intersection. The medic sat next to me.

"We don't need to go so fast," I said, not liking the sliding around. The snow was flying faster now. "Am I okay?"

"You're a good patient. You're not screaming," he said. "You woke me up early this morning, I've got my PJs on under my snowsuit."

Not screaming? Should I be screaming? I wondered to myself.

Suddenly we were at the hospital. The medic wheeled me into the emergency room. Once again, I said, "Please call North Branch Middle School and tell them I'm going to be late."

The nurse smiled and said, "Of course," as she cut the pants off my bleeding leg. I felt just fine, I really just wanted to get up and get to work. Home room would be starting, and I wasn't there.

Finally, she asked, "Do you have the number?"

"Yes, it is right there in my purse."

She left with the number and came back saying, "I called. Everything is fine."

Fine, how could it be fine? I wasn't there. Who was going to take care of my class? I didn't get the pies there, I just wanted to get up and go. I struggled to sit up, then my neck felt terrible, I looked at my leg and sank back down on the gurney.

Suddenly, Bob was there, standing beside me in the emergency room. "Shouldn't you be at work?" I asked, totally surprised that he'd come. The nurse or my school, must have contacted him.

"Of course, I'm here", he said, gently taking ahold of my hand. "You're hurt, you've been in a car accident. Why would you think I wouldn't come?"

Tears welled up in my eyes, I was so surprised. He hadn't been there when I was sick after the baby. I hadn't even told them to call him. My entire body relaxed, feeling loved. I knew, *yes, I do have a husband, a real husband.*

CHAPTER 16

Growth
1978-1984

AT THE HOSPITAL, everything was X-rayed. Nothing was broken. My bashed knee was patched, and I was sent home with crutches, feeling lucky. I figured I'd be going back to work after Thanksgiving. Mom came and made Thanksgiving dinner, but Friday Bob drove me back to the doctor because my neck refused to move. The diagnosis was severe whiplash which meant I had to wear a neck brace: no lifting, no vacuuming, physical therapy, and no work. Staying at home for a month was the recommended treatment. To my surprise Bob helped me every minute he was home until I was well enough to be super woman again.

The next week Bob drove me to the impound lot to look at the car. It shocked me; the front was totally crushed-in like a closed accordion. That I'd been pulled alive from that thing without even a broken bone was a miracle. The Honda was totaled, and we got another larger car to replace it. But my younger brother, who towed cars, said, "Had it been any other brand of small car, you would have been dead".

I was happy to be home with my daughter, who could now walk, so I didn't have to lift her. My wonderful sub who'd been there during my pregnancy agreed to come back for my students. After that month at home, I thought I'd recovered completely, but the after-effects are still felt in the arthritis that permeates my neck and my back to this day

When I returned to work, I found the after-effects were not limited to my body. The drive up to North Branch to teach was terrifying, especially if it snowed. I gritted my teeth and drove anyway, but I started looking for a job closer to home.

Bob managed to find a professional job as a planner for a telephone company. He and I completed the two years of Growth Group at St. Mary's. We now felt comfortable with each other at home. I remember one time we started yelling at each other, but I don't remember why. Suddenly at the same time we stopped. "Is this important?" we said aloud. No, it wasn't and instead of yelling we gave each other a hug. We'd gotten used to our weekly trip to St. Mary's, and we were afraid of stopping.

Our weekly sessions were ending abruptly. This program, which was run by trained volunteers, had gotten us back together. We learned to talk to each other about feelings. Bob respected that feelings were real, not just something to be dismissed as illogical. We enjoyed going every week, so we applied to be trained as Growth Group Leaders. We were accepted. For eight weeks we drove the hour's drive back into the city for training sessions.

In those sessions we learned the theory of group therapy: All personal growth as well as damage comes through one's relations with the significant others in one's life. Emotional social, intellectual, and spiritual growth can take place by encountering oneself and others in the group as real, genuine, and empathic human beings showing unconditional positive regard. We'd seen unauthentic human interactions and knew what damage they had done to our lives, now was our chance to do the opposite.

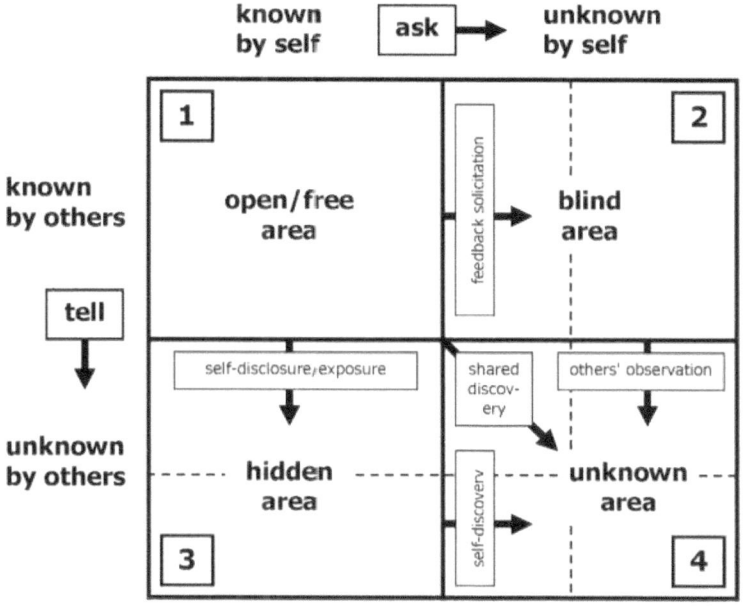

Johari Window

To help us understand group dynamics, the instructors taught us about the Johari window which is a model used to show how trust can be acquired, by showing information about oneself to others and learning about oneself from the feedback of others. Our role as leaders was to facilitate the group in giving feedback to the other members about their interactions. We learned how to deal with other people's problems, but not our own.

At the end of the eight weeks we graduated, and we were given a group to lead. The program directors wanted Bob and me to lead separate groups, but we insisted on leading a group together. Our explanation was that we didn't want to make the hour drive all the way into town on separate days. There was another reason, we knew, but we didn't mention. Growth Group had been our weekly date and we wanted to keep it going. It was a time of deep interaction, not just going to see a movie or out to dinner, but an hour's drive each way, just the two of us, then working together in the Growth Group to help other couples.

Our group met on Friday nights. We got a babysitter scheduled to come every Friday night no matter what the weather and drove into the city. One snowy night we slid in on slippery roads, only to discover that none of the group members who lived closer than us had ventured out in that snowstorm. We laughed, thinking they were just chicken shits, as we drove back home through the blowing snow, but looking back we were probably the dumb ones. Membership varied depending on who showed up, usually the group consisted of 5-8 couples. We led the group for seven years, people coming and going, but one couple, Paul and Diane, stand out as a testament to the strength of this approach to treatment. Paul walked into the group the first night with that stiff held-in look of a man deprived of his usual cocktail, but his wife Diane, was just ugly. Her faced was pinched into a continuous scowl that would probably crack and fall down in pieces if she ever smiled. Each session began with everyone checking in about how their week had been. After two or three groups, Paul had spoken, but Diane hadn't said one word. We encouraged people to just say "pass" if they didn't want to talk that week.

Paul said, "I just couldn't believe it, Diane just left a knife sitting out on the counter. How could she be so careless? What was she thinking?"

I asked, "What are you really angry about?"

"Why didn't she just put it in the dishwasher?" Paul asked.

Another man in the group asked, "Why didn't *you* put it in the dishwasher?"

Paul's eyes turned and he stared at the other group member in shock.

"What was so important about a knife left on the counter?" Bob asked, his voice calm and reassuring.

"How were you feeling at the time? Did you remember to use HALT and ask yourself if you were Hungry, Angry, Lonely or Tired?" I asked, quoting the acronym that we'd discussed the week before.

Paul's face softened. "I'd had a terrible day at work," he confessed.

Diane broke her silence and tears flowed down her face and said, "I was so scared, you were so angry all the time. I just couldn't open my mouth."

Paul said, "I didn't know you were scared."

Diane's strained face started to relax. As the weeks passed, the ugly tension lines melted, and smiles appeared on her face. Beneath that cold strained exterior, a beautiful woman was slowly revealed. Now, 30 years later, I still receive a Christmas card with an original poem composed by Diane and a few notes about the children and Paul.

Not every couple achieved this amount of success, but many made significant progress. One couple split up, the alcoholic didn't come anymore, but his significant other continued to participate for the entire two-year program.

Over time Growth Group changed. While we still had couples, some people came alone. I remember Melissa. She came alone, a pretty, bouncy young woman, sure that this time she'd been cured. Her curly hair circled her face like a halo, and her eyes sparkled when she spoke. She'd been in and out of treatment programs since high school. She came every week for six months, telling stories of her life. She'd worked as a stripper, and said she'd been in treatment with Prince during high school. Suddenly she didn't come anymore. She called us at home, crying into the phone, "They locked me up. My family put me into the Anoka State Hospital, they can't do that."

We listened and went to visit her at the hospital. They let her out to walk the grounds with us. We listened. She said, "I'm okay, I don't need to be here. I'm going to get out next week.

The next week we still didn't see her or hear from her. I called her number. A strange voice answered, "Who is this?" the voice demanded.

"I'm her Growth Group leader from St. Mary's. I just wanted to know how she was doing."

"This is her sister. She died last week. She got out of the hospital and checked into a motel and took the pills. We buried her yesterday."

"I'm sorry, so sorry, we all loved her, she was a beautiful soul," I said, my heart sinking in shock. I couldn't believe all that beauty was lost to the world.

My confidence was running high. We'd been running the group for about six months. I felt I could do anything. I still hated the commute to North Branch, so in the summer of 1979 got an interview with the alternative school program called "Focus" at Kellogg High School, north of St. Paul in Roseville.

It looked like a perfect fit. My first teaching job had been high school students at the Juvenile Detention Center. Surely this wouldn't be much different. The interviewers thought so too.

I was hired.

Before school started, the school board had a lovely lunch for the new teachers. I met Ms. Sanderson (not her real name) at the luncheon. We talked about my previous teaching experiences and how I was looking forward to helping the students in the Kellogg Focus program. These kids needed a second chance.

This program was nothing like the school program at the Juvenile Detention Center. The students came in off the streets. They'd been kicked out of regular school, and this was an alternative. They often arrived at school drunk or stoned. Focus kept them at school and did not send them home. For me it was a nightmare, like facing a class full of drunks. They even threatened to slit the tires on my car. After two months I dreaded coming in at all. I'd stare at my lesson plans, unable to do anything. I discussed the problem with Rick Beresford, who had been the counselor for Bob and me at St. Mary's. He could tell that for me to keep my sanity I would need to resign from this job. But I knew to resign in the middle of a contract could totally end my teaching career.

This program was enabling these students to continue their addictive behaviors and was not helping them or the school. Along with my letter of resignation, asking to be released from my contract, I wrote a letter to the woman I'd met on the school board explaining why I was resigning:

Dear Ms. Sanderson:

I am writing this letter to you because I remember speaking with you at the luncheon for new teachers this fall. In this letter I will attempt to clarify things which I alluded to in my letter of resignation which should be presented to the school board at the November 8 meeting.

I would like to make it clear that I have no personal disagreement with any of the people with whom I worked. I found all of the people I worked with to be dedicated professionals.

The program I referred to in my letter of resignation was the Focus program...By placing students whose main goal in life is to be stoned together and shortening their assignment to meet their shortened attention span, chemical abuse is being encouraged.

(In my opinion) this chemical abuse leads to the paranoid behavior, which results in the physical and emotional destruction of the school itself. Specific examples of this destruction would include such incidents as: the burning of the Focus building (two years ago), dropping of LSD in a teacher's coke (last year), this year, the breaking of the doors on the Focus building three days in a row, tearing down of the railing to Focus building, breaking off a young tree in the courtyard, and in the mainstream school building spray painting "Get Nuts" on the doors and sidewalk, tearing

exposed water pipes off the wall in the rest room, and destroying audio visual equipment.

We can no longer afford to ignore this problem. Education is too precious and expensive. I cannot sanction its being destroyed by a minority of sick individuals of whom some misguided people say, "but we can't deny them an education."

My suggestion to the school board and to the State of Minnesota, is that schools be given the same authority as employers to insist that a student deal with their drug problems (through treatment etc.) or be expelled from school.

Through the In-school suspension program the school district has made a step in the right direction, however that program treats just the behavioral symptoms and once again ignores the probable cause of the behavior.

Sincerely yours,

Patricia Stierna

Along with this letter Richard Beresford included a letter requesting I be given medical leave prior to my resignation to attend a weeklong aftercare program for families of alcoholics. I was an emotional mess.

The program at St. Mary's restored my self-confidence and gave me hope. The school district granted my resignation, and I went back to the University of Minnesota placement office to look for another job. There was a shortage of special education teachers at the time, and the next week I went to a job interview for a job working with elementary-aged children in the Anoka Hennepin School District. I explained very clearly why I had resigned from my previous job and to my surprise I was hired immediately.

Four years flew by. I was happy teaching elementary-aged children. I was able to be creative in my job. I even got to write a book for my students about their classroom guinea pig. Bob was happy in his job as a planner for the Continental Telephone Company. We hired a young girl to help clean house, but I still did all the cooking and most of the childcare, and gardening. Bob took care of the lawn.

I didn't like the idea of our daughter being an only child. I talked with Bob about having another child, but he didn't seem to be able to answer me. I was almost 35 years old. It was now or never. One night I simply announced, "I don't care what you do, but I'm not going to practice birth control anymore." Bob had never been the one to practice birth control, so within a month I was pregnant. Conceiving a child was easy the second time around. I did a home test and placed the results on the mantel of the fireplace

After nine months, I had a C-section to take out my precious little boy. My first child had been born via C-section, so this was protocol at that time. The doctor thought he was ready - after all I'd been pregnant for nine months, only poor little Alex was not ready. His lungs weren't developed, and he turned blue while he rested on my breast. They rushed him away to intensive care. I pumped my milk, wanting so badly to nurse my little boy. He was over 9 pounds. I'd told the doctor I'd carried Alice 10 months, and my mother carried me 10 months. Why didn't he listen? I stayed in the hospital, visiting intensive care at night holding my poor little boy. Mom came and held his little finger when I was too tired to do it. After a week he started to breathe normally. He was breathing, and I could relax and breathe too. We all went home together.

When Alex was almost two and Alice was six, my Jewish friend, John, asked me about taking the children to church. If I wanted them to learn about God, it might be a good idea to find a church. I wanted them to understand the ideas behind "Let go and let God."

The image of Christ had been there and helped me in India, but I hadn't thought of joining a church. Christ was a personal image, not one defined by a church. I looked around my neighborhood and found a Lutheran Church that felt okay to both Bob and me. I loved the music and the feeling of belonging as we sang and prayed together as a family. I'd never been baptized, and the children hadn't been baptized either. I was embarrassed by not having been baptized at a child, so we had a private ceremony. John agreed to be my son's Godfather, and Bob's brother and his wife were Alice's Godfather and Godmother. At the ceremony we joined the Lutheran Church. The pastor couldn't help but tell the congregation about our lovely ceremony that included a Jewish Godfather.

The art teacher at school said his church was having a Christian art show. I decided to make a painting to enter in the exhibition. I danced outside using my paint brush and oils on a three-dimensional canvas supported in the back by a cross that a neighbor stretched for me. Leaves were falling off the trees as I created the painting. It showed the image of Christ that I saw in the mountains of India. One of my favorite hymns was *Now the Green Blade Riseth*, and the painting depicts the changing of the seasons with the green blades coming up from between the branches of a tree with falling leaves. I gave the painting the name "Resurrection". It didn't make it into the art show, but it now resides in the entryway of my church.

Now we had all the trappings of a perfect family, two parents and two children, a boy, and a girl. I should be happy. I worked hard, and we still went on Fridays to help others in the Growth Group.

At home I was still trying to be Superwoman. I did all the laundry, and all the cooking and was getting totally worn out.

Bob bought a new power boat. Everyone in the neighborhood admired it. Dick, who owned the bar said, "Of course you can afford that, you stopped drinking."

Bob insisted we go out early and rake the leaves in the yard, so he'd be able to go fishing and not worry about it. Out there, raking the leaves with him I felt anger building up in me. The only work he did around the house was mowing the grass and helping rake leaves. He wasn't interested in me or the children, that was all *my* job. I was angry, but I didn't tell him I was angry. We were able to help other couples communicate but our communication seemed to be shutting down.

We had a good roof over our heads, and we had food on the table. Bob didn't go out every weekend and get drunk like his father. My mother had never worked outside the home while my father was alive. I'd never seen how a marriage was supposed to work. The image I had of my mother and father interacting was my mother having dinner on the table when Dad came home from work. I got home from work first, so I tried to provide that.

Life seemed like an endless drudgery for me. Every day I rushed to the babysitters and picked up the children. Then I rushed home to make dinner, and after making dinner and washing the dishes, I ran the water in the tub, and bathed the two children. I put on their jammies, read them a story and lay down while they went to sleep. I often fell asleep with them. Bob sat at the computer working on something, but I wasn't sure what. He didn't come to bed until I was asleep.

CHAPTER 17

Al-Anon
1984-2008

AFTER SEVEN YEARS as a Growth Group leader telling other couples how to get along, I was unhappy. Alice hated the babysitter we had coming on Fridays, almost as much as when she'd screamed, back when Bob was drinking. I felt guilty leaving her each week. Yet there were very few babysitters available in our neighborhood. I just couldn't do this anymore. We quit leading the Growth Group at St. Mary's.

I told Bob, "I want a divorce."

His eyes grew wide, "Why, why? You have a roof over your head? I'm not drinking. Why would you want a divorce?"

"I'm tired, and I just can't do it anymore. I'm living a lie," I said, thinking I married the wrong guy. Yet I hated myself for saying it - he looked so hurt.

I didn't want to admit my motives. I didn't even realize how worn out I was. I thought I'd made a mistake and married Bob on the rebound. I never really dated; I just went from Masayoshi to Bob. Reading my own ideas and frustrations into the *Course in Miracles*, I convinced myself that Bob was not my 'soulmate'. A 'soulmate' sounded like the perfect solution to my endless days.

It was the early 1980's and divorce was very common. Women were finding liberation. Baby boomers had the highest divorce rate of any generation. Divorce was so common that my eight-year-old daughter thought it would be fun to have divorced parents, like her friend who got to go to two Christmases. I even talked about getting a divorce with the minister at the church we'd joined; she was young, not married. I remember she said, "You have choices." I had choices, and my own income, choices my mother had never had.

I was hysterical. In bed I screamed at Bob, "Don't touch me," as my whole body stiffened up, frozen, unable to really speak.

We separated in the same house. I moved my bed to a finished room in the basement where I'd written my thesis. I needed to find myself.

My mind and emotions put me into a traumatic flashback; it was like he was my brother trying to touch me. If he wasn't my soulmate, it wasn't right that he should touch me. My feelings raged out of control.

Alice was eight and little Alex was only two - not a good time to have their parents divorce, if there *is* a good time. Bob and I went into counseling again. He went to a men's support group, and I went to see a female counsellor. She diagnosed me as having PTSD. She helped me put my feelings into words and learn to ask for what I needed. But I still had no sense of who I was as an individual. I wasn't very hopeful. After all, we'd done this before.

Bob was still willing to do anything to keep us together, but he didn't cry and carry on like he'd done when he was drinking. He joined a men's support group. He changed; he became more outgoing, ready to talk about things with other people. I was still trying to find out who I was, what I might be able to do on my own, or where I might find a soulmate After three months of my insisting that I wanted a divorce, he brought a friend from work home.

The sun was shining brightly as he greeted a dark-haired thin woman in the driveway. "Hi Cathy. Did you have any trouble finding the place? I'm so glad that you could come."

I'd followed him out, always happy to meet visitors. He turned towards me. "Patsy, this is my friend, Cathy, from work." She held out her hand, and I shook it.

Letting go of my hand, Cathy ignored me and looked into Bob's eyes. "No problems. Your directions were perfect. Such a pretty place," she said as her eyes took in the little house, and the sparkling blue lake just across the road.

"Hi," I said, trying to get a word in edgewise.

Cathy turned back towards me, "Hi," she said stiffly. She obviously hadn't come to visit me. I felt like crawling into a hole to disappear.

Bob said to Cathy, "Let's go for a walk along the lake."

Our house faced a little dirt road that went along a lake. The autumn leaves were starting to fall. A cool breeze ruffled my hair as I turned to watch them go, their backs facing towards me. Cathy's hair bounced as she walked. She reached over and touched Bob's hand. He took her hand in his.

I stared at them. My teeth clenched together, and my heart raced. I was filled with rage. *What is it? What's going on?* My mind raced to catch up with my body. I'd never had an intense feeling like this.

I looked away and collapsed down on the grassy hill that led up to the house, holding my head in my hands. My mind reeled 360 degrees. *It's jealousy, isn't it?* My body was telling me something that my mind didn't want to know. This man loved me with all his heart. He was the father of my children, and I - I loved him, too. He'd always been there for me, except when he was suffering from the disease of alcoholism. In fact, he never looked at another woman. If there was a good-looking woman on the street, I'd say, "Isn't she a ten?"

He'd say, "What's a ten?"

He never seemed to care to even look at another woman. I never dreamed I'd feel jealous. I was a free spirit. I wasn't possessive. We'd been together since I was 19 years old; he was my rock that I depended on. Maybe, just maybe, we could still work it out. I walked quickly the other way along the lake, hoping Cathy wouldn't stay long.

I didn't come home until after I saw that her car was gone from our driveway.

Bob told me Cathy's sad story, "She's been a widow for almost a year. Her husband died of a brain tumor."

"Oh, that's too bad." I said, summoning up my ability to feel empathy, only too aware that I wasn't ready to give her my husband, sad story or not.

Jealousy made me realize that my soulmate might be right in front of my eyes. Later that night, I told Bob, "You know, I think we can work things out, I don't think I want a divorce." But I never admitted to those overwhelming feelings of jealousy.

We stayed separated in the house and I got serious about working on myself. I joined an Al-Anon step group. I learned to reach out and have women friends. I did an Al-Anon fifth step with a counselor and felt relieved of burdens I had carried for years. Despite working with a counselor before, I still carried guilt from my childhood, and my infidelity. A fifth step is a type of confession to admit to God, myself, and another human being the exact nature of my wrongs. I learned that when I surrendered my defects of character, I could let go of things I'd done in the past and find within myself assets I never knew I had. I learned to like myself and that having empathy and listening to others was an asset.

In addition to counseling, we went out on dates or to the movies. We eventually went together to an Al-Anon and an AA meeting in Anoka. It was a true courtship

After six months it was almost Valentine's Day, and we decided to try a second honeymoon. We hired a different babysitter whom the children liked, to come and watch the children while we flew away to Arizona. The jet plane whisked us away from the cold snow of Minnesota to warm, dry sunshine. We rented a convertible. The warm Arizona wind blew my hair as we searched for the home of our dear friends Pat and Nick. They left the yoga group when we did and had a son a little bit older than our kids. We found their old stucco house, that was naturally cool. They gave us hugs and a private room all to ourselves. They showed us Saguaro National Park. We even did a quick trip to Mexico. By the end of the week, I knew I'd made the right decision. Bob was my soulmate, and the father of my children.

We flew home arm-in-arm, our hearts flying so high we could have flown without a plane. Our old friends reminded us of our shared history, and we knew we wanted to create more shared history.

As soon as we made it to the house, we presented the children with gifts. They rushed into our arms. The gifts dropped on the floor, unopened. Tears welled up in my eyes. I was so lucky to have two beautiful children and a husband who loved me.

Thirty years later in 2008, I was asked to be the Al-Anon keynote speaker at an AA Convention. At these conventions an AA person and an Al-Anon person each give a speech that shares their experience, strength, and hope. I worked on my speech for nine months but never told Bob what I was going to say.

Sometimes he peeked around the corner at me, sitting at my computer working on it, and I'd say, "You'll hear it when I speak it. I'm not going to show it to you before then."

He'd just nod his head and walk away. To practice speaking in public I read some other things that I'd written at a local open mic talk. These were funny things, and I got a laugh.

In that two-hour speech I shared my experience with Swami Rama. The audience laughed when I got to that part of how Swami Rama convinced me I was his wife from a previous life. Having done the stand-up talks at open mic, I was able to laugh with them – it was pretty funny. Then I got serious. I shared Bob's treatment at St. Mary's, then I shared my part in our near divorce. And how Al Anon helped me through all of it.

"I learned in Al-Anon how to listen to others and how to have women friends. I knew about my experiences, but I needed more than anything else to listen to others, to learn from them. I learned how to have confidence in myself, and to share my experience, strength and hope without telling others what to do. I still had problems, but I could share them with my Al-Anon group. When I had problems with work or with my children, I shared them with the group, and they helped me work through them, not telling me what to do, but listening and helping me to listen to my own inner voice.

My son understood. When I was too worried about him, or when I started to seem controlling, he said, "Have you been to your group lately?"

I try to work the AA steps in all my affairs. (The bold type lists the steps of AA and the description is my personal interpretation as explained in Al-Anon).

Step 1. Admitted we were powerless over alcohol—that our lives had become unmanageable. I am powerless over other people. I can share my experience, strength, and hope, and my opinions, but then I work on letting go. My life is not manageable without my higher power. I go with the flow. I was not anxious to give a speech here, but a speaker was needed, and I knew I had a story to tell. I have worked and prayed about this for many months, writing my first draft nine months ago and turning it over to God, and trying it out on a few close friends.

Step 2. Came to believe that a Power greater than ourselves could restore us to sanity. For me that power has been a presence in my life and a guiding light since I stared into those mountains in India. When I have strayed from the path, that inner voice, sometimes speaking through friends, has led me back.

Step 3. Made a decision to turn our will and our lives over to the care of God as we understood Him – or, as my dear Al-Anon sponsor in Minnesota would say, as we understood God, not liking to assign a gender to God. For me the words are not important, it is a visual image of light and a feeling in the heart, not a name in words.

Step 4. Made a searching, fearless moral inventory of ourselves. When I worked through the blue book (a pamphlet that helps one do a personal inventory), it was a great agony. Today I try to look at what I do and have done each day—often forgetting, but I do try to do what I feel is right. Writing this speech was a BIG 4th Step.

Step 5. Admitted to God, to ourselves and to another human being the exact nature of our wrongs. My first 5th step was very difficult – telling my husband I was sorry and telling someone about my experiences as a child and a young woman. Since then, I have taken little steps, trying to correct errors as soon as I become aware of them. Often this is at an Al-Anon meeting, or in this speech. It is not easy to lay my life down here; I am not proud of everything I have done, but I feel there are things unspoken that need to be shared.

Step 6. Were entirely ready to have God remove all these defects of character. I continue to have defects and the best cure is to "Let go and let God."

Step 7. Humbly asked Him to remove our shortcomings. I love the reading in Al-Anon that talks about feeling like Swiss cheese. God removes those defects and only holes are left. The big discovery is that in those holes are assets and knowledge gained by pain.

Step 8. Made a list of all persons we had harmed and became willing to make amends to them all. In writing this BIG 4th step speech I realized my brother Dennis was a teenager too, a physically ill teenager. I can forgive him and forgive myself.

Step 9. Made direct amends to such people whenever possible, except when to do so would injure them or others. I would not have spoken about my brother, except that he has died, and his lovely wife who adored his memory has also passed from this life. I have made amends to those I could, including my husband and my mother, although she could not understand how I could possibly share my problems with other people. She never did learn how to trust people. Sometimes it is not possible; some things are best left unsaid, or perhaps the people involved simply cannot accept your apology. A friend tried to apologize to the wife of a man she had an affair with; the apology seemed to cause more pain than relief, at least for the wife—for it was the wife who told me about this.

Step 10. Continued to take personal inventory, and when we were wrong, promptly admitted it. I try to do this every day, or at least every week. I hope that today I have not taken too much of your time, and that sharing my story will help you on your own journey.

Step 11. Sought through prayer and meditation to improve our conscious contact with God as we understood God, praying only for knowledge of His will for us and the power to carry that out. Attending church gives me a quiet place to reflect and meditate, allowing me to get in touch with God as I understand this presence; also, to practice hatha yoga, but not raja yoga under the direction of a guru.

Step 12. Having had a spiritual awakening as the result of these steps, we tried to carry this message to others, and to practice these principles in all our affairs, which is why I am here today.

In Al-Anon I am able to "Let go and let God." I listen to that inner voice, and peace descends. Some people get confused by this concept of God, but in AA the advice is to try letting go and listening to your own inner voice.

Bob and I continued to work on our marriage. We learned to unhook and travel through this life side by side. We were hooked like this (showed fingers hooked together). Now we are like this (traveling fingers side by side).

On our 25th wedding anniversary, we had a big party and renewed our wedding vows at St. Martins on the Lake Episcopal Church. Everyone came, and everyone participated. We were happy we knew now our marriage would last for the rest of our lives. Rain poured down during the ceremony. The reception was to be at our house, in the yard. As we left the church it was still raining, and over 100 people crowded into our three-bedroom rambler. The sun came out and we all went outside. Friends set up their band in the garage. We insisted they play the Beatles song, "When I'm 64," and we danced the first dance to this song. The picture on the front of this book shows our joy.

Our daughter was a difficult teenager when we had that party, but she sang during the wedding ceremony. Years later, on Bob's 64th birthday, we received a phone call from the post office. They had a package for us, so I went to pick it up. It was mailed from Austin, Texas at a cost of $40 for Sunday delivery. *What on earth was our daughter wasting that much money on to mail to us?* I thought. I brought it home and Bob opened it. We hugged and cried at the thoughtfulness of our grownup daughter. In the package was a silly frog holding on to a walker singing, "When I'm 64."

It is easier to explain the pain and relate horror stories than it is to share pure joy. Each day I wake up thankful for my life. The sun shines, the rain falls, clouds roll by. Sometimes things come up from my past. I just came across someone on the Internet trying to find information about Swami Rama. I responded, and it did not bother me to talk about what happened to me so many years ago, even knowing that there were things I tried to stop. I have faith that in the end the good will win and each of us will learn that the most important things are to be truthful and to listen to one's inner voice.

I find comfort and sharing in a Christian church. Being raised Unitarian, I cannot say that it is the only way, but it is the way I have found that works for me. Being at church and coming to Al-Anon help me to stay in contact with God, and to Let go and Let God.

I know in Al-Anon we do not give advice, but I would like to give these words of advice. Everyone knows the old saying: "If life gives you lemons, make lemonade." Well, after being raised an organic gardener, and gardening myself, I say, "When the world gives you shit, make compost, and grow!!"

As I gave the speech, Bob stood in the back of the room. I had not shared any of it with him. The speech was my apology, for my part in our near divorce. I stepped from the podium to a loud applause, and Bob raced up to give me a hug. There were tears in his eyes, "I never knew, I thought it was all my fault, but I didn't know what I'd done wrong."

Tears filled my eyes. I knew I had wronged him. I hadn't admitted my part in the near divorce. I didn't tell him what it was I needed. I just asked for a divorce. I knew all was forgiven as he put his arms around me. We hugged each other, so happy to have stayed together. The audience gave me a standing ovation from the arms of my husband.

CHAPTER 18

The Healing Network
1990-1997

Just before Christmas 1990, I watched the snowflakes fall gently outside our picture window. In the distance I could see ice boats darting back and forth on the frozen surface of Lake Minnetonka. They whizzed back and forth enjoying the very short period of clear ice before the surface would be covered with snow. When we'd moved here in 1987, our neighbor from Coon Lake, our previous home, had said, "You're moving to paradise."

I laughed and said, "I don't think so, I'm not ready for heaven yet."

The truth was that the view from that front window was heaven on earth. Every morning I watched the sun rise over the lake and gave thanks for our life. It was a Saturday morning, as I relaxed, staring out the window, the phone rang in the kitchen. I picked up the receiver and heard a voice from the past.

"Hi, this is Debbie. How are you doing?" the voice said.

"Debbie?" I asked searching my memory. "Oh of course, Debbie from the yoga group." My mind finally found the right storage cabinet. We'd stayed in touch over the years through Christmas letters. She was a medical doctor now. "Just great here. How are you?" I asked, surprised to hear this long-lost voice from the past.

The wax started to melt on that sealed cabinet of memories. all the failed attempts to do something to stop the continued abuse of women by Swami Rama. *At least I'd kept Kimaya out of his grasp*, I thought.

Debbie got right to the point of her call, "Did you see the Yoga Journal article?"

"No, what's it about?" I asked. I'd been too busy with my life to pay any attention to the yoga world.

"The Yoga Journal, a very respected national magazine just published an article by Katharine Webster called **The Case Against Swami Rama**," she said.

"Really, thank God, maybe it will make a difference," I said, feeling that maybe this would stop his continued abuse of women. I remembered what I'd said to Swami Rama in India, seventeen years earlier, when I promised not to talk. I told him in a spoken vow, *If I hear you're doing things again I will do everything in my power to stop you.* I'd tried. I spoke out in 1974, when my friends had shared their stories of abuse. I told my story to the FBI guys. Yet almost nothing had changed.
Oh yes, Swami Rama had changed the center of his operations in the USA from Chicago and Minneapolis to Honesdale, Pennsylvania, but that was all.

"I'll go pick up a copy, do you think they'll have it at Target?"

"I'm sure they will, I think I saw it there," Debbie answered.

"Thanks so much for calling me, maybe this is finally the beginning of the end of this," I said as I hung up. All the memories started to bubble up like a nightmare that never ended.

I got my coat on and headed straight to Target. As I pulled the car out of the garage and drove out into the falling snow I thought, *Maybe someone finally saw the truth and he could be stopped.* I drove down our long driveway and turned left onto the busy little two-lane road that separated our home from the lake. As my car emerged from Highway 15 onto the freeway, I saw a snowplow clearing the road. I hoped somehow this article would clear the road, providing a path to finally get Swami Rama out of the country.

I got off the freeway, fighting my way through both the traffic, and crowds of people in spite of the snow. The parking lot was full of holiday shoppers. Christmas was fast approaching, but I wasn't interested in buying presents. I just wanted that magazine. Large snowflakes melted on my hot cheeks as I swished through the revolving doors into the store.

I went directly into the magazine racks. *There it is*, ***The Case Against Swami Rama*** was headlined on the cover. I grabbed it and headed to the checkout. Afraid that I might start sobbing when I read it, I didn't open it until I got home.

At home, I sat down at the kitchen table and opened the magazine to page 59. I stared at Swami Rama's picture, so innocent in a maroon robe wearing a knit hat. My stomach turned in revulsion at the very sight of him. I hated reading the story, yet I knew I must persevere. I'd ignored this for too long. He had not kept the promise he made in India. To keep my promise, to do everything in my power to stop him, I needed to know what he'd been doing for these last sixteen years.

It was all too familiar, the same stories of women trying to justify his abuse, wanting to believe it was all for their enlightenment, only to finally realize that they had been abused. They tried to tell the people running the Himalayan Institute, but they were shunned and dismissed as being emotionally disturbed. My eyes zeroed in on Katharine Webster's description of the Jungian psychologist, Peter Rutter, PhD, and his analysis of "sex in the forbidden zone." Yes, that was me. We'd all been seduced by this guru, violated, and our trust in God and ourselves betrayed. Could the laws that had been passed since the acceptance of this concept be applied to a guru? The guru wasn't regulated by a professional organization like doctors and psychologists, or even a religious institution like a church, but maybe it could still apply.

The author wrote, "The victim's confusion and loss of trust is compounded when her community refuses to acknowledge her suffering."

My blood started to boil. "Refusal to acknowledge" doesn't begin to express the heartbreak of excommunication and being labeled a hysterical female lusting after a "poor celibate swami".

Luckily, I'd had family and friends who'd supported me through that experience seventeen years earlier. At the Honesdale campus of the Himalayan Institute, the women were isolated from each other, and the rest of society while being abused by Swami Rama. My heart ached for the women described in the article, especially Carolyn's story. It was just a continuation of what I and other members of the Meditation Center tried to stop in 1974, only on a larger scale. Now he had more money, more power, and more women. I needed to do something; I needed to reach out to these women.

The article did clear the road and start a path. It started before I'd even seen the article. Kay, the head of the Meditation Center in Minneapolis, resigned. Her letter of resignation said that Swami Rama's history of sexual misconduct had been around for a long time; it mentioned the Menninger Foundation, and the women who'd been abused. The Meditation Center in Minneapolis was tied to the Himalayan Institute, so she had to resign.

My heart reached out when I re-read the letters written by Jim, who was with us in the beginning. He dedicated years of his life to the Meditation Center in Minneapolis. I remember when he lived at the Center, a thin blond-haired young man, with eyes that showed a compassion beyond his years. We were shocked when he refused to believe our stories that we told him so long ago. But in 1991, with the Yoga Journal article, the ice melted, and his eyes were opened to the mind-manipulation used to close everyone's eyes. He could no longer deny that women were being abused, and he questioned why others continue to deny the abuse. He wrote, "Are all moral issues to be dealt with by using one's practice of meditation as a means of settling the mind and not taking action?" Or maybe those in denial just, "see these accusations, if true, as a flaw or a paradox that does not affect their personal relationship to the Teacher or teaching."

I went further than that: I said these leaders lost empathy, they were high, and their minds were manipulated into their own personal state of joy, so fuck the women - whatever happened to the women was for their own good. Those in denial were simply unaware, and unable to see the abuse. Some victims too were in denial of their own pain, believing that this is all part of their instruction.

But the Himalayan Institute (HI) continued to deny and attack its accusers. The head of the Institute issued a letter to the Honesdale residents and staff stating that the article is "deplorable and misguided." Dr. Arya was flown in solely for the purpose of telling the Honesdale members, gathered in an emergency meeting, that they shouldn't pay any attention to the article and that their confidence in Swami Rama should not waver. Honesdale sources reported that in a remarkably brief period of time the HI administration silenced almost all discussion of the article. Sources inside HI said "People are afraid to discuss the article, knowing that to do so will indicate that they give it some amount of credibility. Then people will suspect them of infidelity, and their life and livelihood, which is with HI, will be at risk."

Meanwhile, I completed the school year, concentrating on my job and my family. When summer came, I organized a gathering of concerned people at my home on Lake Minnetonka. It was a wonderful gathering of old friends, and Debbie helped me find the names and addresses of people who had been involved. I typed out an invitation and mailed it to anyone whose address we could find; plus, we called everyone whose phone number we still had.

The day came, and the weather was perfect. I was excited to see these people again. The meeting time came and went, but nobody had shown up. It felt like nothing was going to happen but finally, my phone rang, "We're in Wayzata, but we can't find it."

"You left the highway too soon. You have to keep going until you get on Highway 15." I redirected them. Finally, our driveway filled up with cars, and my arms and heart filled with hugs from long-lost friends. A writer, Nancye Faulkner Belding, interviewed me at the gathering. It was becoming so depressing, yet it still continued. I wondered, *Why even write about it? Why was I telling my story?* I reminded myself: *The laws have changed. Maybe justice could stop this abuse.*

Bob was a gracious host, keeping the coffee cups filled and the children entertained, while I talked with these old friends. Jim came; he finally gave up on trying to separate the Meditation Center from the Himalayan Institute, and instead helped found the Healing Network.

We put up notices and sent out flyers trying to contact victims of abuse by swamis. Here is the first flyer:

THE HEALING NETWORK
IS SEARCHING FOR GOODWILL AMBASSADORS.
AS AN AMBASSADOR YOU WILL
HELP IN PREVENTING SEXUAL ABUSE IN SPIRITUAL
COMMUNITIES
HELP IN EDUCATING THE PUBLIC ABOUT THS ISSUE
HELP VICTIMS IN THEIR HEALING
HELP IN FUND-RAISING FOR LITIGATION
PLEASE WRITE TO JIM YOUNG AT THE HEALING
NETWORK
P. O. BOX 6908 CHAPEL HILL NC 27516
*NOTE: THE HEALING NETWORK IS ASSISTING
TWO YOUNG LADIES IN THEIR SUIT AGAINST
SWAMI RAMA AND THE OFFICERS AND DIRECTORS
OF THE HIMALAYAN INSTITUTE.*

The flyer asked people who'd been abused to come forward and asked for contributions. I signed up right away.

Two women, J. Patel, and M. Heinze, were moving forward with a sexual abuse case against Swami Rama and the Himalayan Institute. Patel was just 14 when he started training her to serve him, and when she was 19, he took her virginity. The story she told was vile and despicable, a young innocent girl sent to the Himalayan Institute by her parents, then coerced by Swami Rama into secret sex with him.

These women needed all the support we could give them. I didn't care if I got anything out of the suit or not. Jim and Prafulla Patel, the young girl's mother, approached me to be Vice President and secretary of the Healing Network. I didn't have much extra time because of work and young children, but I volunteered, nevertheless. I was determined to stop this abuse forever. Everyone else they asked to take an active role in the Healing Network declined, because many were afraid of retaliation by the organization.

Letters of support and donations started pouring in from around the world. I received letters from California, London, Washington State, Minnesota, Arizona, Okinawa, Japan, and Illinois, all offering support and many included checks to help pay for the litigation. Through this organization I finally reconnected with Kimaya. It was Kimaya that Swami Rama had been seducing in 1973, and she was the main reason I confronted him about his sexual abuse of women. I saw in her eyes a blind devotion that I felt would lead to serious abuse by him. Instead of saying directly to her that I'd been seduced by him, and my friend had also been seduced, I confronted Swami Rama about it, and just hinted about it to her. In 1973 she'd even written me a letter saying that nothing happened between her and Swami Rama. I wondered if he asked her to write that letter, because now it all came out. 1973 was the beginning of years of abuse that did not stop until she left the center in 1980, but even then, was still associated with it. She didn't speak out until after the Yoga Journal article. The story she told made my blood boil.

In her letter to the HI dated February 1994, she describes how she was seduced, still in her teens. She wrote:

"I was frightened, shocked, and confused at his overtures toward me. I told him that I did not want to have a sexual relationship with him and that I just wanted to be his student, to learn meditation and yoga from him. He said that this was not possible. He began to convince me that refusing a sexual relationship with him would be the same as turning away from my spiritual path. I even began to feel guilty for not wanting to do what my Guru was asking me to do. I was afraid that my life would become troubled if I did not follow his counsel. And so, I entered into a relationship that consisted of five years of sexual abuse.

This was not a relationship based on mutual consent, but a relationship based on psychological coercion. He used his position of power as my spiritual teacher to exploit and control me. He would often tell me that as a person I was "imposing" because of having sex with him. He said it was "my therapy" and I believed him. He told me that this was a very special sacred relationship and that I should never tell anyone about it.

Although the physical abuse was damaging, the psychological abuse was even worse. Like other abusers, he would vacillate between praise and hyper-criticism. Always keeping me off balance. At times he would humiliate me publicly or ignore me for months at a time. He would scream at me for minor mistakes. At those times I would blame myself and think that I just wasn't a good enough yogi - not meditating enough, not constantly remembering my mantra enough. Over time, my self-esteem eroded..."

Every time I read that letter, I said to myself, *See where being nice gets women? No, instead of hinting at things, I should have gone right out and said that he told Pat, he told me that we were his wives in a past life, that we were the only ones.* Maybe that would have made a difference, but then maybe not. I was still being manipulated in India when I thought I'd had the upper hand and I had confronted him.

It was Kimaya's letter that finally got the director of the Himalayan Institute to begin to question his guru. In December 1993 he wrote a very carefully worded letter to the institute directors saying that Rama's behavior should be investigated, because Rama involved himself in a way that students considered abusive. Even if this was done for some good reasons we cannot understand, it could be damaging to the institute and the work that Swami Rama gave to it. He felt that confronting this behavior would be showing respect and the mission he had started. It was not showing disrespect or lack of caring, but rather concern for him and his mission.

However, in his letter the director totally forgets to acknowledge that Swami Rama's behavior hurt the women.

But even more damaging than that was the response of the organization to this letter. The leaders of the institute simply accused him of trying to take it over, and destroy it. By March 1994 they were intent on attacking him. He responded finally, calling for an investigation into the allegations of sexual misconduct, but his pleas were ignored.

On June 6, 1994, Kimaya wrote to me asking me to write to a lawyer, Lori Peterson, who was interested in pursuing a class action suit against Swami Rama and HI. Kimaya asked me to tone down my initial letter because it was too emotional for the legal community. On June 22, 1994, I rewrote the letter detailing my abuse, and subsequent counseling I'd received. I also mailed certified copies to the board of HI so that all members would know of Swami Rama's abuse.

In August 1995, Jim was served a notice as the President of the Healing Network that an old friend of his, Rolf of the Himalayan Institute of Buffalo, New York and the Himalayan International Institute was going to sue the Healing Network and its officers, which included me. I was aghast, I knew I'd not only put my reputation on the line, but my very life, I didn't have any funds to use to defend myself against a lawsuit. Jim confronted Rolf in a letter. Jim ended his letter with these words: "I assure you that my (and others') meagre assets will bring you neither restitution nor comfort. Nor will they dissuade my intention to continue efforts to bring to light what has happened and stop any future abuse. My hope is that you have not fully joined the forces of revenge and denial which we both know have existed throughout."

In September 1995 I was still hard at work as Vice President/Secretary of the Healing Network I wrote a letter to Janet Reno the Attorney General of the USA. I also sent copies to Senator Wellstone, my Minnesota senator at the time, and to the FBI. Nothing came of these letters.

In October 1995, the Healing Network received a final blow. We were denied tax-exempt status, because one of our goals was to raise money for the lawsuit. Jim called me, and we decided to dissolve the organization. None of us had funds to fight a lawsuit, and we didn't have time to fight this refusal of tax-exempt status. But we both knew we would do anything to help the suits against Swami Rama to continue.

The lawsuit against Swami Rama was filed in July 1994. Swami Rama was served with the complaint in India. Swami Rama denied that he had engaged in any sexual contact with the plaintiffs and denied that he had ever engaged in any sexual activity with any female disciples or students at the Himalayan Institute. He refused to cooperate in the trial, or to be represented by his attorneys. However, the case against the HI was allowed to continue with a trial set for spring or early summer 1997, and I was one of the possible witnesses.

I was excited when the lawyers contacted me as a potential witness. Finally, someone was standing up to this man, and this organization that had allowed this to continue over all these years. The trial was set for August 11, 1997. This was during my summer vacation, so it would be easy for me to go. The lawyers said the trial would take four to six weeks of testimony and they would be calling approximately 30 witnesses.

Unfortunately, as the date neared, I was informed that they would not be allowed to call any witnesses prior to the Himalayan Institute moving to Honesdale, Pennsylvania. I was heartbroken. I'd quit the yoga group and any association with the Himalayan Institute before its center of operations moved to Honesdale, Pennsylvania. I wouldn't be able to come to be a witness, but I was hoping that they would win.

Swami Rama died in India in 1996, but the trial, since it was also against the organization of the Himalayan Institute, continued. I wished he'd lived and come back to face the court, but I hoped there was justice beyond this life. The Institute tried to settle out of court, and one plaintiff settled for $125,000, but the Patels refused $350,000, they had been treated too badly, so it continued to trial.

I was elated when I heard that they won. In a jury trial they were awarded $1.6 million, with $275,000 in compensatory damages by the jury. I'd like to say Bob and I had a celebration, but we didn't; we just had the joy of continuing our lives together.

Then I heard the Himalayan Institute appealed.

I was sure with Swami Rama dead, they probably never got anything. I didn't hear the final results of the appeal. No one contacted those of us who held our hand up to testify with a final vindication.

CHAPTER 19

Retirement
2007-2010

I QUIT THINKING ABOUT the trial and all the yoga stuff. I was beyond all that, into everyday life, working, celebrating birthdays, and holidays, especially Christmas. My husband and I always had a traditional American Christmas. When the children were young there was an early church service with the children on Christmas Eve. Christmas Eve dinner was celebrated with Grandma and the uncles along with an exchange of small gifts.

When we opened the door of the house on Christmas Eve, the smell of the real pine tree dominated the entire house. The children ran into the living room and checked the tree to make sure it had water, then they touched the few wrapped boxes that were sitting there ready to be opened in the morning. They made sure their stockings were hung with care above the fireplace, even the pets had stockings waiting for Santa to fill during the night. Then they put a cookie on a special Christmas plate, and a glass of milk on the coffee table for Santa.

Once the children were in bed asleep, Bob and I got to work. Bob was the perfectionist; he was the one who wrapped each present; even the ones from Santa that went in the stocking. They had to be carefully wrapped in Santa paper. It was often past midnight when Bob took a quick bite of the cookie and drank the milk. Then we collapsed into bed, hugging closely, as we snuggled in anticipation of Christmas morning.

We'd hardly closed our eyes when the bed started to bounce up and down. The children were champing at the bit, and wide awake. "Wake up, wake up, its Christmas. Santa's been here," they chanted as they bounced. They knew they needed to wait just a little bit longer. Daddy needed some coffee, and there was a picture to be taken, a picture to help us remember this special day. The youngest child passed out the gifts, one at a time...

But this Christmas it was 2007, and the children were all grown. My Mom had died in 1998, and Bob's mother and father were gone too. The elder child, Alice lived far away and was celebrating her 10th wedding anniversary with her husband. There were no grandchildren yet. My younger child, Alex, had a room near the university and was helping us finish moving the contents of the house where he'd grown up. I'd already been retired for almost a year, and we'd moved to Door County WI, while still trying to sell our life's investment, our home on Lake Minnetonka.

We'd managed to buy a small apartment building with four apartments (a four-plex), three to rent out and one for us to live in. Door County, a peninsula surrounded by Lake Michigan had everything we dreamed of doing in retirement. Sailing was Bob's passion and I loved being first mate, raising the sails and recording our experiences in film and pottery. The large lake gave it a slightly warmer climate, so pursuing my passion for gardening would be easier than in Minnesota.

But now, after two years of that house being FOR SALE, we were teetering close to bankruptcy. We kept lowering the price, praying. I even buried a statue of St. Joseph in the yard as suggested by a Catholic friend. Finally, it sold. The closing was going to be December 27, 2007. We had two weeks to move out. Alex took pictures and posted everything on Craigslist for us. The two white love seats, with scratches from the cat, the modern style lamp with a spiral post, the heavy desk from my office all were carted away. We kept the paintings of mine and my mother's, our books, and the plants many of them gifts from my mother who'd died in 1998.

The old Christmas stockings were all packed away. There wasn't a Christmas tree. I said to Alex on Christmas Eve, "We're going to exchange presents at Uncle Gene's house tonight."

"No, no, I am not going to open any presents tonight. Present are opened on Christmas morning," Alex said.

"What do you mean? We don't have a tree. There is nothing in the house, not even a couch," I answered in shock. I knew it was tough on him, but he had been so grown-up, so helpful.

"I am not opening any presents at Gene's house," he repeated, with tears in his eyes.

"Okay, but we are". We left his presents in that almost empty house.

At my brother's house, the Christmas tree was covered with lovely decorations. The couch was comfortable and the dinner delicious. Alex recovered and played the role of the older cousin to the younger children. Even the three dogs managed to get along with only a few growls. We returned home and went to bed to continue packing up the house on Christmas Day.

I woke up at 5:00 a.m. on Christmas Day, as is my habit every day. I proceeded into the almost empty living room to do my morning exercises, when I noticed that things were out of place. A cardboard box had been moved and leaning against it were three Santa Bears in a row. I sat down on the one remaining chair and noticed two pieces of my favorite bread sitting there along with a glass of milk. Looking around the room, I saw three shoes sitting on the fireplace hearth with Christmas wrap showing out of each one. In the corner where the Christmas tree always stood was my large hibiscus plant with Christmas decorations hanging from its branches. Flashlights lit up the plant. Under this plant were beautifully wrapped presents for my husband and myself.

My mind finally made the connection. *"It's Santa, it's Santa,"* remembering the chorus the children sang on Christmas morning. I ate my favorite bread, savoring every bite, for there was not a single cookie in the house. I ran to the bedroom to get our presents for Alex and place them under this lovely tree.

My eyes filled with tears of joy. My son was a grown-up man who remembered the traditions I taught him.

After that lovely Christmas morning, we worked frantically, filling a rented van with the rest of our belongings, and cleaning the house from top to bottom. The house passed its final inspection, and we went to the closing and signed paper after paper, sitting side by side. Bob squeezed my hand as we waited for them to print out the check. They handed us a check that contained the results of a lifetime of work. Bob carried the check in his breast pocket and drove immediately to the bank, to put it in safe keeping.

We were so relieved that it was sold that we didn't miss it at all. The beautiful view wasn't necessary; the new kitchen Bob had built himself wasn't necessary. All we wanted was peace of mind and time: time to live, time just to be, time to be retired.

Moving in Minnesota in December is never easy. After we signed the papers Bob got into the rented van, and Alex followed driving the car with me in the passenger's seat and our adopted mutt Stella in the back. Stella wagged her tail happy to be traveling with the pack. She looked like a small German shepherd, but she was all love, never growled and very rarely barked.

As we pulled out of the driveway buckets of snow started falling from the sky. The road wobbled in and out of view through the flashing windshield wipers. Whiteness dominated everything. The only reassurance was the sound of the tires rolling on the pavement. Alex and I slowed down, keeping a safe distance behind Bob in the rented moving van. We held our breath as we watched the van slide towards the ditch.

Years of winter driving reflexes came into use. Bob turned into the skid and the van swerved back the other way onto the pavement. Before the next exit Bob turned on his blinkers.

"He's turning off the highway, maybe we should stop for the night," I said, relief allowing my tense jaw to relax, and the car followed Bob up the exit ramp.

"Great idea". Alex said, his white knuckles clutching the steering wheel.

We hunkered down in a motel to wait out the storm. The next morning, we awoke to blinding sunshine reflecting off piles of whiteness glistening all around us. During the early morning hours, the snowplows had cleared the highway. As we drove across Wisconsin, we counted twenty cars in the ditch, counting our blessings that we'd missed that experience.

Once at our new home Alex helped us unload the moving van and he took the bus back to Minneapolis. As soon as we finished unpacking we volunteered based on our personal interests. Both of us took an active role in the local AA and Al- Anon groups. Bob took up teaching boating safety and navigation with the Power Squadron, and I trained to become a Master Gardener, and a volunteer naturalist. I took on keeping invasive plants out of a city park known for its rare wildflowers. Garlic Mustard was taking over and would quickly crowd out all the wildflowers. Stella loved coming to the woods with me staying close while I pulled weeds. In the garden she even helped pick off potato bugs until her white muzzle was smeared in bug juice and she was sick of it.

During our long, retired nights our bodies functioned as one. Breaths matched in unison. If our old bodies decided to merge in sex, years of practice gave us amazing grace. We climaxed together, a oneness of being in light that brought closeness and delight. Lying next to him, breathing in pure joy, a cloud of worry passed over. *How will I ever live without him?* I'd already almost lost him twice, once during a routine polyp removal after a colonoscopy and then replacement of his defective heart valve. But he was well now, and I was so happy we were together.

With a little extra money from the sale of the house we splurged and bought three things. We paid cash for a new 2500 Chevrolet Diesel Silverado from the local Chevy dealer. Because of the housing collapse, it was one of the few cars they sold in 2007. This beautiful cherry red pick-up truck was big enough to pull our sailboat, and had a truck bed large enough to hold a slide-on camper. We drove down to Green Bay and purchased two matching Stressless chairs, a large Papa chair for Bob and a medium sized chair for me. To me they seemed outrageously expensive, but beautiful in their simple lines and ergonomic design to support the spine. The Ekhornes of Norway Stressless Recliner is advertised as the most comfortable seating in the world.

Later we purchased a used camper and traveled south during the winter, but summer always brought us back to Door County, gardening, and boating. Our boating friends had never been to Lake Superior; they'd just boated on the warmer, calmer Lake Michigan. We said, "Don't worry, we've been boating there a lot, we'll all go together, and we'll show you the ropes."

We met in a parking lot, our boats on trailers and set off for the Apostle Islands on Lake Superior. Later that day we were launched. Taking off from Bayfield to Stockton Island, we in our sailboat, Compromise, and our friends in their power boats we ran into high winds. We all got tied to the docks on Stockton and walked across the island to Julian Bay for a picnic on my favorite pure gold sand beach, the winds howling the whole time. After our picnic the power boaters decided to go back to Bayfield and wait for calmer weather. As they pushed off from the dock, the winds clocking 15-20 knots, a friend yelled, "Be sure to speak at our memorial service," since I was the official prayer person for the local Power Squadron that year.

I answered, "Be sure to stay with the boat, whatever you do, and you'll be fine." Bob and I were sure our sailboat would be able to handle the 10-20 knot winds predicted for the next day.

We awoke early and sailed towards Raspberry Island Lighthouse, one of our favorite destinations. There was a bit of a blow, and the waves were beginning to roll. We took off from the dock and raised our sails. Looking up at the mainsail Bob noticed a small hole. The winds seemed to be increasing beyond 20 knots. "We'd better go back and get that fixed," Bob yelled above the gale.

I didn't want to climb up on the deck in that wind to take down the sail, so we decided to motor sail back to Bayfield. The motor started and we turned the boat into the wind. The waves started to swell, and the motor strained against the wind. All of a sudden, we heard a loud clunk, and the motor stopped. Bob turned the boat using the sail to keep us upright. "Check for water coming in," Bob yelled.

I opened the hatch, looking down by the motor. I didn't see anything. Bob had me take the wheel, something I hated doing. I liked being first mate, but keeping that boat on an even keel was not easy - it always wanted to slide off course. I struggled to keep the boat from turning sideways and rolling over, dumping us into that icy water.

Bob stuck his head down near the motor. "We're taking on water," he said. He dug in the storage compartment, pulled out the hand pump and started pumping. I struggled to keep the boat sailing into the waves straight on. Bob's arms were getting tired, and we were taking on water faster than the little pump could handle. There were islands nearby but sinking into the cold waters could cause death after only ten minutes. He called the coast guard in Bayfield on the radio, "Pan, pan", he called, "We're taking on water," and gave our precise location.

I thought, *What? Isn't this Mayday? We're sinking*. I stayed at the helm, and he pumped and pumped. Within 10 minutes the coast guard boat appeared. They knew it was Mayday. A little coastie hopped on board. She inspected the situation and took over the pumping, her young arms much stronger than Bob's. Bob took back the helm. Our dog Stella checked her pockets for treats, keeping balance easily with her four legs on the rolling boat.

I grabbed my movie camera and started filming, the best way to keep myself calm and out of the way. The coastie called for a boat to pick us up and her boat towed our sinking vessel back to Bayfield. As she pumped, she explained that this was her first rescue.

Later I produced a YouTube video which can still be seen by googling Apostle Islands Rescue, pstierna. This is a much better film than your usual vacation narration. In the film you can see Bob shaking his head. He had trouble accepting that he missed a precaution he'd taught every boater to take. That ended up the most exciting vacation of our 10 years of sailing the great lakes. Bob hated the video though, not liking being recognized when the boat was being repaired in Sturgeon Bay. I left it on YouTube, but it was never presented to the Power Squadron as the educational video I'd imagined it to be, since Bob was unhappy with it. Love always requires compromise.

CHAPTER 20

Angels Along the Way
2011-2016

RETIREMENT WAS A JOY, but problems always crop up. That's life. My younger brother said, "You're living the retirement dream, you know."

I laughed and said, "Yah, but we don't get our weekends off," which was the truth. We worked, especially on weekends, because other people needed that time off to be with their young families.

Bob and Alex built a pottery studio for me in our basement, and on weekends I sold my pottery at the local farmer's market. Bob did free boat-safety inspections with our boating group, the Door County Sail and Power Squadron, or worked at West Marine, the ultimate store for boating supplies. We usually took the sailboat out during the week when there was less traffic.

It was a lovely summer weekend in 2011. Earlier in the week Bob had a successful surgery to remove a cancerous growth in his colon that they'd found during a routine colonoscopy. The doctors assured us they'd got it all. He wouldn't need radiation or chemo.

I was confident that he was doing well, so I joined the traffic heading north to Sister Bay where I'd set up my pottery for the Door County Art League annual show. I imagined the lovely little angels I'd made in clay with leaf-shaped wings. Each one had been made with a prayer of hope and thanks. I counted my blessings. *I'm blessed it's not 1955. It's 2011 and they know how to deal with this. He's not going to die of colon cancer like my father.* The truck slowly proceeded, going less than the posted 55 miles per hour on the crowded narrow two-lane highway My thoughts stopped when my phone rang, but since I was driving, I didn't answer it. It rang again. I pulled over to the side of the road and dug it out of my purse as it continued to ring.

"Thank God, you answered, I hurt like hell," Bob's voiced cried out from the phone.

"What is it?" I asked. "You sound terrible. Do you think it's a problem from the surgery last week?"

"I... I don't know; it just hurts, burning, just a burning feeling. Like a hot poker in my gut."

"Okay, I'm coming right home."

I turned the truck around, squeezing into the traffic going south, its slowness driving me crazy. Maybe he should have called the ambulance. Finally, I raced in through the door, and saw him sitting in his Stressless leather chair, his face drawn and white, his wisps of white-blond hair shining from perspiration on his forehead.

"Let's get you to the emergency room," I said, as I helped him walk out to the truck. We'd purchased a house in town just so we'd be close to the only hospital on the Door County Peninsula - it was only a five-minute drive. When we arrived, I dropped him off at the door and squeezed the truck into the last empty spot in the parking lot. Almost every seat in the emergency room was occupied. Sirens roared as more people poured in - accidents, too many tourists, they said. We waited, Bob sitting there in burning pain, and we waited some more.

While we were waiting, I called my artist friends. They sold my angels for me and packed up at the end of the show.

Bob didn't have a broken leg or a smashed pelvis, just pain - terrible pain. It was at least four hours that I stared at the clock and watched my husband sit there in agony. Finally, there was a break in the traffic accidents, and they called Bob into a room.

They felt around, examined his healing scar, and declared he had a kidney stone. I couldn't believe that after that long wait all they did was send him home with more pain pills and a strainer to pee into to catch the stone when it passed. But at the same time, I was relieved that he could go home, and not back into the hospital.

After 24 hours of pain, he passed the stone, and the pain eased. I was amazed that such a little thing could cause so much pain. Once again, I gave thanks that he was still at my side.

Bob was going to be okay. I didn't need to worry about him. Everyday Stella and I walked over to Marie Vandenhouten's house. She was a 90-year-old widow, a state I hoped I'd avoided for now. Marie lived on her own in the home where she and her husband had lived. When I knocked on the door she'd say, "Oh, so nice to see you," and invite us in. She'd been happily married for 70 years, but she said, "I just never was blessed with children." She shared a wedding picture with a perfect 1920s outfit, the short skirt and the straight short hair under a lovely hat shading her beautiful smile, that smile still showed through the wrinkles on her face. When my children came to visit, I made sure they stopped by and visited her too.

As soon as I heard the news that my daughter was pregnant, I raced over to tell Marie, "I'm going to be a grandmother, I didn't think it would ever happen. She said not to tell anyone, but I know you won't tell."

"Of course, who would I tell?" she asked, laughing, sharing my joy. I knew she didn't know any of Alice's friends in Texas.

As Alice's due date approached, I made plans to be there when the baby arrived. Bob was going to stay in Wisconsin, and I was going to drive my car down to help with the new baby, then he would come down later with the truck and the camper. This way I'd have a car there. I was nervous and excited. I'd flown to India on my own, but never driven on a three-day trip alone. I confided in Marie, "I'm 65 years old. That's old enough to drive to Texas on my own."

Marie was totally shocked. "Are you sure that's safe? Why, we never even drove outside Wisconsin. We started on a trip once, my husband driving of course, but we turned back - it was just too far."

"Of course, it's safe," I said. "Maybe you haven't traveled far across the land, but you traveled through time further than most of us," But I hoped now I could learn to be more independent if I ended up a widow.

I made it to Texas with my own car. I was doubly blessed, unlike my mother's mother who'd died when my mother was twelve, my mother was alive when my children were born and now, I was going to be with my grandson. He was in the ICU for a week, and I went to hold him every day, until he got to go home.

For the next three years we spent every winter in Texas with our grandchildren - one and then two grandsons. Bob loved the boys and dreamed of teaching them how to sail and play baseball, his favorite sport. Every summer we were back into Door County sailing and volunteering. We made plans for a big trip during our 50th wedding anniversary year which was coming up in 2017. I told Bob, "Let's go back to Australia. I will have finished my book about my mother's life and her paintings. We can share it with my family there."

Bob said, "I want to go out West in the summer like on our honeymoon."

I said, "Why not do both, drive a smaller camper across the Rockies to San Francisco and then catch a boat to Sydney. It would be the opposite of the trip Mother took in 1923."

"Sounds, like a plan." Bob said, always willing to compromise.

Then in 2014 cancer hit again. They were monitoring Bob every year to check for a recurrence of the colon cancer. His blood levels were up which meant the cancer might be back. They did a scan; it was back now, in his liver, Stage 4, they said. We saw a surgeon in Texas - a specialist, who told us they can operate on livers, which grow back. Then he showed us the scan on Bob's liver. "I'm sorry," he said as he pointed out that Bob's cancer was in three spots." I can't operate on that. It is too spread out. The oncologist will say you have longer, but I'd say you have two years if I can't operate."

Bob walked out shaking his head, "How can he say that. I'm sure it's not just two years. I'm going to fight this. I'm not ready to leave yet." I didn't say a word. I hoped Bob was right. I wasn't ready to be a widow. I didn't know how to be alone, or do anything on my own, except drive to Texas.

For two years he took every drug they could prescribe for colon cancer. He saw a woman oncologist in Texas during the winters and a male oncologist in Sturgeon Bay in the summers. The doctors monitored his progress. He took exercise classes and continued to work at West Marine in the summer. He got progressively weaker. In late August, we went to the oncologist at the Door County Medical Center. The oncologist said, "We've exhausted all treatment options; there is nothing more we can do. You will need to go into hospice."

My heart wanted to stop beating. I'd known these drugs weren't working but wasn't there something better than this?

I watched Bob stare at him; his jaw clenched in contained anger. Surely there was some other treatment. He was writing a proposal for a new national lakeshore park - he needed more time to work on it.

"No," he said to the doctor, Bob's gaze much stronger and more determined than his body.

I steadied his balance as we walked out of the clinic. He said to me, "I want to see my oncologist in Texas. Maybe she can find some other treatment. I'm not done here yet. I'm not ready. I'll never leave you."

I nodded my head in support, but I felt a sadness in my chest that made each breath seem heavy.

We left the clinic and I drove us home. He needed a nap. I lay down beside him, breathing with him. Chemo allowed no sex, but as we shared air in unison, I wished to love him into wellness. Love through the years had bonded us, so caring for him was not a burden. Though the doctor had indicated the end was near, I wasn't ready for it either. I was terrified of being left alone.

It was the tenth summer that we'd sailed *Compromise* on Lake Michigan. We needed to get the boat out of the water and into storage as soon as possible so we could hurry down to Texas to try to get some other treatment. Our friends could sense the desperation in my voice when I asked, "Could you help us take the sailboat out? Bob is worse and he wants to get down to Texas and see his oncologist in Austin."

Bob was so ill he could hardly walk. He watched from the passenger seat of our Silverado truck. His pure blue eyes were pools of sadness that did not cry. *Would he ever sail again?*

Our friends - Bill, Steve, and Craig from the Door County Sail and Power Squadron motor sailed *Compromise* up to the dock. With Bob's encouragement I backed the truck down the ramp. I watched while our friend jumped into action, walking out on the trailer, and clipping the cable onto *Compromise*. Craig, the youngest in our group, cranked her up onto the trailer. I put the truck in gear and pulled her dripping body out of the water.

Then we had to take down the mast. I could feel Bob's misery watching us. This was his baby, and I was sure we weren't doing it right.

"Just take out the pin," I said, pointing to the pin at the bottom of the mast. It held the mast upright.

Craig pulled on the pin, but it didn't budge. I went below and grabbed the multi-tool.

"Here, use this," I said, handing him the plier's part. After a couple of wiggles with the pliers, the mast wobbled loose. We all held onto the guy wires and slowly lowered the mast to the deck. With the mast down and the guy wires tucked onto the deck we strapped it onto the trailer. After thanking our friends, I put the truck in gear and towed the boat to its winter storage.

Bob sat in the passenger seat, muttering to himself, "I don't know how I'll ever straighten those guy wires out again."

"I'm just glad it's out of the water," I said, thinking *I will never sail without him,* as I held back my tears.

Bob, while hanging on, hoping for a cure, worked hard to push me towards independence. He showed me all the computer passwords and tried to teach me his complex accounting system. We bought a mower that was easy for me to start and push. Every step of the way I'd wanted to close my eyes. *No, no, this isn't happening. I don't want to do this.*

With the boat out of the water and in storage, I needed to figure out how to get back down to Texas.

"I don't want to be here when it starts snowing," Bob said. His eyes teared up in desperation.

Since we'd been blessed with grandchildren, we'd spent the winters in a Fifth Wheeler camper in Austin Texas, on the shores of Lake Travis.

These campers are called 5th Wheeler because the trailer hitch is a wheel installed in the bed of the truck just like in a big semi-truck rig. This spring we'd pulled a 40-foot 5th Wheeler up to Wisconsin. Maybe we should have left it in Texas; during the drive up it had blown a tire and the tire had ripped the paneling. It had been at the repair shop of our local camper dealer all summer.

I knew how to drive the truck, but I'd never driven it when it was pulling a trailer, or a boat. Bob liked to be in charge of that, and I was happy to be a passenger. Now he wasn't capable of driving. Pain medication made him fall in and out of sleep.

I am woman, I am strong, I am invincible. In desperation I hummed the line from Helen Reddy to myself, while I thought of who could help. I really didn't want to try to drive the truck pulling that house-sized camper down to Texas. I talked to some neighbors about helping me drive it down. They were willing, but then I thought maybe Alex, my son could help. I called him. The next week, Alex and I were at the local camper dealer, picking up our repaired Redwood Camper. It looked fantastic, with new siding, and new tires. In the parking lot Alex got some lessons on driving the truck with this huge camper attached. I felt proud of my son, taking the reins. He'd always been the baby, but now he had really grown-up.

It was just our second day of the trip. Alex was feeling confident, and I was enjoying riding in the back of the truck with Stella, our dog. Bob sat up front in the passenger seat, falling in and out of sleep. Suddenly a trucker passed us and slowed down right in front.

"What the hell!" exclaimed Alex, surprised by this reckless behavior of a semi-truck.

I leaned forward from the back seat. The trucker continued to slow down in front of us.

"He's trying to tell us something is wrong," Bob said.

"Yah, we'd better pull over," I said, crossing my fingers that it was just a mistake.

Alex gradually slowed down and pulled over to the side of the highway behind the trucker. The trucker walked back to our truck. He said, "I saw a tire rolling off into the meridian about 12 miles back. When I passed you I saw your tire was gone. You're lucky you didn't roll."

Astonished, we walked around the camper. There on the rear driver's side, where there should have been two tires, there was only one carrying the full load. The decorative fender was ripped up again. I paced up and down, all of the muscles in the back of my neck tightening up.

I managed to open my mouth. "Thanks so much for stopping us," I said, as he hopped in his 18-wheeler and took off down the highway.

I dialed the roadside assistance number inside the camper door. "Press 1 if you need roadside assistance," an automated voice said.

I pressed "1".

"Press 7 if you are stranded on a highway."

I pressed, "7".

The phone went silent. I was cut off.

I started over.

Tapping on the phone, fingers flying in frustration. Finally, a ring, then the warning, "This conversation may be recorded."

My thoughts racing, *Who cares?* Finally, a human voice full of static wanted my roadside assistance number. I read it off the side of the door. Then they wanted the make, then the weight. I didn't know the weight.

Finally, the voice said, "Okay, we'll look up the weight, and I'll call you back.

The phone rang as roadside assistance called back, and said, "We can't find anyone nearby. You have $300 service on this policy, anything beyond that is out of pocket. You would need to be towed since you drove without that tire for 12 miles."

The traffic whizzed by on the highway. An Illinois trooper named L. Ormond pulled in behind us and where the tire had been. "This is bad, but I know a local guy who can help you."

The remaining tire and the body of the camper were not seriously injured; the hub had not touched the ground. No way was I going to be towed. *How could I care for Bob if we were towed? Where would we stay? His medication, everything was in the camper.*

"Never mind," I told the operator on the phone, totally disgusted. Then turning to Officer Ormond I said, "Let's get your local guy. My husband is ill, we need to get this fixed."

He called Allen's Tire and Towing in Pittsfield Illinois. "They are sending Greg; he should be here in half an hour."

Officer Ormond helped us slowly drive one mile to exit 10 and off to the side of the exit ramp, safe from the dangerous Highway 72 traffic. I helped Bob get from the truck into the camper to use the restroom. While I was caring for Bob, I heard action outside the camper. *Is Greg here already?*

I got out and there was Greg, an angel with a torn shirt showing tattoos up his arms. He quickly jacked up the hub and removed it, showing strength and knowledge of all things mechanical. As I watched Greg I was reassured, remembering my father's strong arms. The bolts were broken off in the hub. He tried to get them out. "I didn't bring the right tools," he explained as he pounded, trying to get the bolts loose, but only 2 out of 8 popped out. I suggested using the bolts that came out to push out the others, but they weren't the right shape.

"Oh, I'll go work on it at a shop only 8 miles away. I'll be right back."

Greg returned with tools and managed to create a hub with 5 bolts to hold the spare, which he wrenched loose from beneath the camper. Once the spare was on he asked us to slowly follow him to Pittsfield along the back roads where they could try to find us a new hub tomorrow.

We stopped along the way and Greg checked that the tire was holding. We followed Greg to Allen's Tire shop. We turned in behind the shop on a gravel lot covered with tires and equipment, unsure how we would get out. Greg went in the office. I followed Greg into the office, which consisted of some unmatched chairs, and papers strewn about, not a bigtime corporate office. It was already past 5 pm. Greg suggested we camp for the night at Jellystone Park on Pine Lakes or the city Campground on Pittsfield Lake. One guy standing in the office said, "The city campground is cheaper, only $15 a night."

It was dusk, as we set the GPS for the city campground that Greg had mentioned. I worried the wheel might come loose at any moment. Alex clutched the steering wheel while his father sat calmly in the passenger seat. Bob saw a sign with an arrow for camping on Lake Pittsfield, but the GPS said keep going and we trusted it, turning onto a small road that quickly changed to gravel - still no campground. The GPS said turn, and we turned onto a still smaller gravel road.

This brought us to a lovely little lake with a tiny road winding through the large trees but we didn't dare go down that road, since it was too small for us to turn around and if we met oncoming vehicle in the dark, there would be no room to pass. Out of the tiny road a car emerged, its lights shining in the dark. I flagged the driver down and asked, "Is there a campground down there we can get to?"

The driver, a small, short-haired young woman with a child in the back, said, "I'm not sure, but I think so." She started to drive off, then returned. "I'll drive down and check it out for you. Be back in five."

Ten minutes later she reappeared, "Yes, there are campers down there. But that road is too tight for you. Let me show you an easier way."

We turned around, following our guiding angel as she turned right through a metal gate onto another narrow road. Alex drove to the far side of the road, carefully turning the big camper through the gate, but there wasn't enough room and we got stuck, even with a few attempts.

A white pickup came along. Instead of yelling at us for blocking the road he said,

"I know a better road for you to take." We waved our first angel goodbye and followed the white pickup. We came to a T in the road, and the driver said, "Turn right here and follow this road across the levee and to a T; at the T turn right and the campground will be there."

We drove slowly through the darkness. Alex kept the camper to the left where he could see the edge of the narrow dirt road. Finally we saw water on either side, the levee, then the T. There were lights. *Thank God, a campground.* We pulled in. *How were we going to find a spot and set up in the dark?* Another angel - Fred, the campground host - emerged from his camper, and set up the water and electricity for us.

Early the next morning my phone rang. Allen's Tire said, "Come over to the shop, and we'll find that hub for you."

"Can't you come here?" I asked thinking of the terrible time we had getting to this campground.

"We need you at the shop, so we'll know exactly what hub and tire to get for you."

"Okay," I gulped out, thinking of the horrendous drive last night. I got out of the camper and asked Fred, "Is there a different way out of the campground than how we came in last night?".

"Oh, it's easy. You just stay on the blacktop and turn right. Eventually you will get to a T that is the highway, turn right again and you will be in town," Fred said pointing to a very nice little blacktop road out of the campground.

We drove back easily to town in the daylight. At Allen's Tire, Greg took off the temporary hub and spare.

We waited and waited as action continued around us. A trucker had a blowout. A farm wife came in asking about fixing a tire. I mentioned how they were helping us. She said, "They are wonderful. They keep us going; we'd be lost without them."

Later, while I was sitting in the truck with Bob waiting, a very kind older man came up to the window. "Where are you folks from?"

"We're from Wisconsin, going to Texas to spend the winter with our grandkids. How about you?" I asked.

"I'm from here," he answered. "I started this shop in 1958. Now my sons run it and my grandson is starting to work here too," he said proudly. How nice it was that he was here to guide his son and his grandsons. I hoped Bob could get through this and be around for his grandsons

The Allen brothers said we could stay there and plug our camper in for the night, but we decided to return to Fred and the lovely city campground on Lake Pittsfield.

America has lots of wonderful local people, I thought. I was amazed by all of the local people like angels, who'd gone out of their way to help us total strangers. I'd paid a lot of money to have roadside assistance and insurance, but it was the local people who were the angels, they made the difference, *Maybe we just need to trust each other and depend less on big corporations like road-side assistance.* I reflected, still amazed at all the help I'd been given.

Back on the road, it seemed like we were through the worst that could happen, but the next day the engine decided to slow down and wouldn't go over 40 miles an hour. We'd never reach Austin at that speed, so we stopped at a station where they cleaned the filter. It seemed like a go, but then the engine slowed again as we neared Mineral Wells, Texas.

"Let's just stop here. Maybe if the engine cools it will be okay again," I said, not knowing what else to do. As we parked near an old hotel. I grasped Bob's weak hand in mine, sending him love and strength. "Alex and I are going for a short walk."

We stepped out into the warm Texas air and walked up to the hotel. It looked like something from the roaring twenties extending high into the sky. It seemed large enough to hold all the residents of that small town. Every door was locked, and an eerie emptiness oozed out from the inside. Ornate chandeliers hung over an expansive room as we peeked in through the bars that covered the windows. A sign said it would be open for tours on Halloween. We laughed about it; after a trip from hell, a stop by a haunted hotel seemed totally appropriate.

After half an hour we resumed our trip. We were almost there, and the truck jerked and sputtered but it pulled us the rest of the way. We stopped at the locked gate next to the carved stone that read, Camper Resort on Lake Travis. My exhausted brain couldn't remember the code. I called Mary Ann and she answered right away.

"I'm so glad you made it. We've all been praying for your safe arrival."

The sound of her voice lifted my spirits. She rattled off the code and I repeated it to Alex. The gate clanged open, and Alex put the Chevy in gear. It lurched forward as we drove through the gate.

CHAPTER 21

Hospice

As we went through that gate, I remember the spring five years ago when we drove down this road looking for a winter home to be near our grandchild. When I saw the gate, I almost turned around, but then I saw a phone number. I called the number and Chuck, an energetic elderly man with thinning white hair, a trim moustache and a ready smile let my daughter and me in. It was an ideal place, just what Bob and I wanted. The camping sites had a view of Lake Travis and were shaded by beautiful live oaks, their leaves hanging on green all winter. Before Chuck had even shown me around, my story burst out of my mouth, "I'm a new grandma. My husband and I are getting a 5th Wheeler so we can spend the winters near our grandchild. I hope you have an opening".

A small woman with short grey hair hanging neatly on either side of her glasses, and a solid no-nonsense figure stepped out to greet us. After a quick introduction, Mary Ellen said, "We don't have any openings".

"We won't be coming until fall. Can I keep checking back to see if anything opens up?"

"Sure, you can, but we can't guarantee anything," Chuck said, leaving the door open a crack.

A month later back in Wisconsin after we'd bought a 5th Wheeler bigger than the little truck camper we'd traveled in earlier, I called again with the same question. I felt like jumping up and down when Chuck said,

"Yes, we do, when are you coming?"

"I'm not sure of the exact date, what do you want for a down payment?"

"We don't need a down payment. Just tell us when you are coming". I couldn't believe this, it was a message, a gift.

I did and we went that fall. I didn't know it then, but I'd passed an interview test. Chuck and Mary Ellen let us into, not just a campsite, but an entire community of caring people.

Those caring angels were there to meet us as Alex pulled the camper forward and stopped in front of our assigned lot uncertain how to back our huge camper into that small space.

I opened the back door of the truck and our aging dog, Stella, jumped out and landed with a thud, wagging her tail. Stella's muzzle had turned white, but her short brown hair still shone bright and inviting. Marianne and Kurt greeted her with a scratch on the back. Kurt was from Minnesota and had visited us in Wisconsin. He even drove me to Minneapolis when Alex was ill. Mary Ellen was all smiles and glad to see us, but her husband, energetic Chuck, had died a couple of years before. Angie's beautiful white hair reflected the sadness of her recent loss, her husband Tommy had died of cancer during the summer. Janie's husband died suddenly the year before, but they all stayed on in this tight community.

Kurt immediately volunteered to back the camper in. Alex slid out from behind the wheel, "Sure, thanks for the help," he said.

Mary Ellen asked Alex, "Are you up for a poker game?"

"Sure," Alex answered.

"We'll all have to watch out for your dad - he's a real card shark" Mary Ellen said, referring to the haul Bob made at penny poker last year. I wanted to shake my head, not knowing if he would be able to play this year.

I'd jumped out after the dog; Bob got out slowly out of the truck and greeted everyone. Our winter friends watched with concern as I helped Bob walk towards the door of the camper, now secure in its winter spot. Alex hooked up the water and sewage and climbed on the roof to put the antenna in place. Bob sat down in his Stressless chair that we'd moved into the camper before we left Wisconsin. Here he could look out the back window onto the lake.

I got our sign out. I'd just gotten it last year. On the left was a sailboat carved into the wood, and on the right a tree. In the center *Stierna, Bob & Patsy* was engraved in the wood. As I hung it up, I prayed that Bob & Patsy would be together at least as long as the wood didn't rot. We'd come so far, Bob and I.

I called Dr. Grotz, Bob's oncologist, and talked to her nurse. Dr. Grotz called us back personally. She would see us next week. Yes, she thought maybe she had something to try. Bob's smile extended from one thin high cheekbone to the other. His dull eyes brightened. There was hope.

I relaxed and started to make dinner. Bob got up and slowly made his way up the stairs to the bathroom/bedroom part of the camper. He came out and started back down the two little stairs. Bob missed one of the steps and before I could reach him, he collapsed on the floor.

Oh shit, why wasn't I watching? Why didn't I help him walk down those bloody stairs? I thought, as I helped him lie down on the couch.

Marianne was a nurse practitioner, I ran out and knocked on the door of her large camper two sites down. She followed me back. Her experienced hands gently touched Bob's hip as he laid stretched out on the couch.

Bob grimaced in pain.

"Maybe he just twisted it". Marianne said ever an optimist. Let's see how it is tomorrow". Together we prayed for him to get better and be alright.

In the morning his hip wasn't any better. The neighbors helped get him into the truck and I drove him to the hospital. I sat in the waiting room, hoping he would be OK. We were called in to see the X-ray.

"His hip is broken, right there." The doctor pointed to the X-ray. The black and white bones showed a definite line, a break. "He will need an operation."

I just sat there in shock; my vocal cords unable to talk. I thought, *How can he survive surgery when he has terminal cancer?" I thought, he's got to survive. He's got to get better. Maybe a miracle?*

They had his chart; they knew he had cancer. The break wasn't caused by the cancer, so they operated. After surgery Bob went into rehab. If he survived that, maybe we could still try the new chemo.

I visited him every day for 82 days. When I discovered that dogs were allowed, Stella came with me. She held her head high, walking calmly beside me, the stockings on her legs a perfect white, her back a light brown with a white collar on her shoulders that extended down to her tummy. She was never dirty; she cleaned her own short fur like a cat. Her claws scraped on the polished floor as she walked. Usually she heeled perfectly so I was surprised when suddenly she pulled me into the room of another patient. "I'm sorry, excuse us". I blurted out, embarrassed.

"No, don't go," the man said as he sat up in bed and petted Stella.

I smiled, thinking Stella would have been a perfect therapy dog. She'd been therapy for both Bob and me.

Bob was diligent and did the exercises to the best of his ability. I watched him walk holding onto railings, while the physiotherapist walked beside him, cheering him on. Bob's grim smile showed that each step caused pain, but he was making progress.

We took him out in a wheelchair on Thanksgiving. The family gathered for dinner in the clubhouse of the Camper Resort on Lake Travis. He was weak, but happy to see the water, and his family.

On the 80th day of his stay in rehab I arrived to find Bob black and blue. He'd fallen out of bed during the night. He couldn't get up, and no one had helped him dress. I helped him get dressed and went to inquire why no one had tended to him.

"This is a rehab center, not a long-term care facility. He should be able to dress himself by now."

I called his oncologist, she said, "I'm sorry, there is nothing we can do. The other treatment was a long shot, anyway."

The liver surgeon had been right. Two years of cancer drugs had taken their toll and not been a cure for Bob. I needed a plan in place before the rehab discharged him.

I called Hospice Austin, a non-profit hospice care organization. "Yes, we can care for him at home in your camper," they said.

I'd missed my mother's death. I'd been at work when she'd died in a hospital facility. I wanted to be next to Bob to say "Goodbye" when he died.

The next day, rehab called a meeting to tell me he needed to leave. I told them my plans, and they were pleasantly surprised that I was ahead of them. They wanted him to leave that very day.

"Wait a minute, I need to get the bed in place first," I told them.

Hospice Austin came out the next day. There was room enough, so they moved the furniture around; and brought in the bed placing it horizontally so that with the head of the bed raised Bob could see out to the lake.

Even though every movement gave him pain, he smiled as we drove onto the grounds of the Camper Resort. I helped him up the few steps into the camper. He loved the bed in the living room where he could look out at the lake.

Stella took up residency under his bed, only leaving when I took her out for a walk. She was also getting old. Sometimes when she stopped to take a leak, one leg would collapse, and she'd fall over sideways. I'd push her back up and she'd be able to walk back home to the camper. The arthritis in her hips had slowly been getting worse, but I'd gotten it under control with large doses of glucosamine.

Alex flew down from Minneapolis, and my daughter, Alice, took time off from work so we could be with him 24 hours a day.

The nurse came and showed me how to give him morphine to ease the pain, and how to move him in the bed, to keep bed sores away. When I turned over his thin body, I could see hard flat white lumps where the cancer was growing on his back. Slowly he ate less and less and slept more and more. Never one to quote the bible, my mind turned to the 23rd psalm *"Yea though I walk through the valley of the shadow of death, I will fear no evil; for thou art with me; thy rod and thy staff comfort me."*

Christmas came, and the family gathered around his bed in the camper. He was as skinny as a skeleton, his pale skin stretched and barely covering his beautiful high cheekbones. His eyes glittered with delight as his grandchildren hung close by, touching him where they could. "Hello Monkey" he whispered in a rasping voice, reaching to tickle the older grandchild as he had always done.

After that day he quit talking. The children joined me at his bedside. They sang "One Tin Soldier" to him, Alex's deep voice blending with his sister's soprano. His cousin, Darlene, drove down from Dallas to say "Goodbye." She looked at her childhood friend who was too weak to talk. Holding his hand, she spoke gently to him. I'm sure he understood each word.

The hospice nurse said he only had a day or two, but he stayed on. He lay there in a coma, neither eating nor drinking. Just his breath continued, breathing in and out. We used a sponge to moisten his lips and gave him pain medication. Another week went by. I sat by him, and whispered, "It's okay, you can go; I love you." Remembering he'd said he'd never leave me. We'd gotten beyond so much together, grown up together. He always was stubborn, his love unending.

Alice, Alex, and I went for a walk, leaving him alone, since we'd heard some people hung on and were unable to die with family present. We came back from the walk to hear his labored breathing continuing.

On January 3, I left him to see a doctor about a constant pain in my gut. I asked my son to drive me; I was too distracted to be safe driving myself. I dreaded being gone and having him slip away without me there.

"Alex, I have a doctor's appointment. Will you go with me?"

"Sure," he answered, always willing to help.

Alice stayed with Bob, and her husband came by to join her. After I finished my doctor appointment, Alex and I stopped in the parking lot of a grocery store. I was just getting out of the car to run into the grocery store when the phone rang. "He's gone," Alice said, gasping into the phone. "He's stopped breathing. We turned off the air conditioner. We can't hear him breathing."

My shoulders sagged and my breathing slowed as I crawled into the passenger seat of the car, so glad Alex was driving. Alex quickly drove home. I rushed in the door and stood over him staring at his still body. His skin was stretched across his face like the white onion skin paper we used to use to write airmail letters. I wanted to yell at him, "Why didn't you leave while I was here?"

There was a deep weight in my chest as I accepted his truth. He wouldn't leave while I was there; he used my little trip to the doctor to slip away, true to the end.

CHAPTER 22

A Celebration of Life on our 50th Wedding Anniversary

2017

SHAKING, I FUMBLED THROUGH the hospice book. What to do next? They had the phone numbers there along with directions to call the nurse and a funeral home. We had agreed he'd be cremated so I called Affordable Burial and Cremations. I knew he wouldn't want a fancy coffin, or a fancy urn. They sent someone out immediately, even though it was getting dark. They came with a stretcher, but they had to put him in a blanket to get through the little camper door.

I felt a deep emptiness. The camper was too quiet. The bed was empty. We hadn't made it to our anniversary. It was only January, and I was determined to celebrate, on June 8th, the date of our 50th wedding anniversary. That would be the date that we would celebrate our life together.

Angie, a friend from the campground, who'd recently lost her husband, drove me to pick up the ashes. Their website advertised that they had the only onsite crematory in Travis County, so I could be sure I was getting the correct ashes. There was no grass in front, no fancy landscaping, just a concrete parking lot in front of a two-story brick building with very few windows. I sniffed the air, wondering if I'd see or smell smoke, and feeling relieved when I didn't. Angie walked with me up the old concrete steps into a dark hallway. They asked, "Do you want to see our urns?"

I took a quick look and said, "No". I wanted to make my own urn - after all, I was a potter. It would be created in his memory with my own hands. They put the ashes in a simple cardboard box. I wrote them a check for $650 dollars, much less than any other cremation service. This way I'd have more to spend on our anniversary party.

The next day we had a potluck memorial gathering in the campground, with our Austin friends. I was already planning the funeral and life celebration for our wedding anniversary, June 8th, in Door County, Wisconsin.

My son Alex stayed on for a few days so I wouldn't be alone. On the third day after Bob's death, Stella came out on her leash for a walk and fell, both back legs collapsing at once. She looked up at me, her eyes asking: Why? I tried to get her to straighten up so she could walk, but I couldn't get her to stand straight. Alex helped me carry her back into the camper - she wasn't a small dog. I called the vet and made an appointment for the next morning.

Kurt and Marianne agreed to go with me to the vet. I didn't want Stella to suffer like Bob had. She couldn't walk, and I couldn't lift her. Kurt lifted her into the truck, and I drove her to the vet. I blurted out something like this to the vet, "I think she needs to go to sleep. She can't walk, and I can't take care of her". The vet examined her and said, "Her eyes aren't cloudy, I hate to put her down".

"But I can't take care of her. I can't lift her," I said. "Besides she'd hate not being able to walk or run. When she could hardly walk, she'd still take off running across the field after a squirrel."

The vet said, "Okay, I understand."

We went into the back room, and I sat on the floor with her head on my lap. The vet inserted the IV in one leg. She didn't even wince as she went to sleep in my arms, my tears falling on her head. I thought how she and I had walked together through Bob's illness, but now they were both gone.

It helped to have a goal; without it, I would have just crumpled on the floor. I had my book, *Visions from Two Continents*, the story of my mother's life, to finish. At every turn, I saw obstacles I didn't know how to conquer, like bills that Bob in his illness had left unpaid, and debts like that on the camper. I couldn't sell it because we owed money on it. I racked my brain trying to figure out what to do. The truck was paid for. I called my credit union in Minneapolis; they loaned me the money based on the truck to pay off the camper. My younger brother, Gene, flew down from Minneapolis and helped me get the camper ready to sell. No one responded to my ads except people who wanted me to pay money for them to sell it. Finally, after two months, my payment grace time on the loan was about to expire; a friend of a friend offered to buy it.

Just one month after Bob had died, I sat down in front of my old Mac computer ready to pick up writing my neglected manuscript. I pressed the on button, but saw only a black screen. I tried again. Nothing. I plugged it in and unplugged it again. I paced the room, took a deep breath, and tried again. My manuscript was in there. I had a backup, but it wasn't all there, I'd been too preoccupied with death, to keep my backups up to date. I got a new computer from the Apple store, and they loaded what backups I had onto it. Then I found a computer geek online who agreed to try to get the rest off my old computer. He succeeded. It was like a resurrection. I felt like dancing when I was able to open my complete manuscript.

It had been such a struggle. I felt relief rather than grief, as I packed up our memories, squeezing them all into the truck. It was already May, time to go back to Wisconsin and get ready for the celebration on June 8th. I drove the truck home all by myself to Minneapolis, and then my brother drove with me to the house. I didn't want to face it by myself.

I threw myself into working on our 50th celebration. I wanted music, someone to play **When I'm 64** by the Beatles, since we'd made it past 64 at least. I wanted lasagna, like we'd had at our 25th. I wanted a service at the church with music and a reception at the Nature Center Cross-roads at Big Creek. With lots of help and love from friends all around, I arranged it all.

On June 8, 2017, I sat in the pew at Christ the King - the tiny church was full. Surrounded by my family, I was free to just give thanks. The church was packed with friends of Bob who'd come from all around. My beautiful daughter spoke of his commitment to staying sober and helping others, while still being dedicated to his family. I was humbled by their presence. As I looked over the program, I noticed something was missing. My mind gave thanks and sang the hymn that was missing. It was a song both Bob and I felt close to:

Amazing Grace:
Amazing grace,
How sweet the sound
That saved a wretch like me.
I once was lost, but now I'm found.
Was blind, but now I see.
(We saw together, we came to love one another)
'Twas grace that taught my heart to fear
And grace my fears relieved.
How precious did that grace appear
The hour I first believed.

The last hymn was there. After the last speaker spoke, we rose together and sang:

Now The Green Blade Riseth.
Now the green blade riseth, from the buried grain.
Wheat that in dark earth many days has lain
Love lives again, that with the dead has been.
Love is come again, like wheat that springeth green.

The gardener in me felt the hope buried in the wheat. It was the embodiment of my painting of The Resurrection, the spirit rising again, through the changing of seasons.

We urged everyone to come to the reception at Crossroads at Big Creek, giving directions at the end of the service. I was disappointed that some people came to one and not the other, but I was blessed by their presence in either place.

Alice, Alex, and I had worked side by side, going through pictures and awards to display at Crossroads at Big Creek. An enlargement of our honeymoon photo from our job in the Lookout Tower so many years ago was placed at the entrance near the sign-in book. In addition to photos, we displayed examples of Bob's professional work. There was the research report he'd written for the Minnesota State Legislature that had given farm workers unemployment insurance. It was an economic benefit to the farmers and had helped farmers have workers to pick their crops. There were future planning reports he'd written for the Continental Telephone Company, not to mention his many volunteer stories about boating safety for the Power Squadron in Minnetonka, and the Door County Sail and Power Squadron.

I was filled with joy as I watched my grandson look at pictures of his grandpa as a young boy. One blond towhead looking at his white-haired grandpa as a little boy.

When the ceremony was all over, I stepped outside the building to see a full rainbow fill the sky. Tears streamed down my face.

Epilogue
2020

2017-2020

I wanted to write our story, Bob's story, and my struggles as a young woman. I brought up the idea of writing this story as I finished writing my first book about my mother, when Bob was still alive.

I thought about the piles of papers I had stuck away in a file drawer, as I said, "You know I ended up with all the material, all the papers from the yoga group; I really need to write that story."

Bob quickly jerked his head towards me; "You can write that after I'm gone." His nostrils flared and his eyes glared in anger.

Oops, that was a mistake. I became very quiet, and let it drop. We had gotten beyond it, but the hurt lingered still. He didn't say anything more about it. We were happy now; I didn't want to bring up my betrayal. I knew he'd forgiven me, but he didn't want or need to be reminded of that terrible time.

I knew he was ill, but I still hoped beyond hope that maybe I'd never be faced with writing this after he was gone. I'd rather just not write it and have him here.

In fact, I wasn't planning on writing this book at all. In the summer of 2017 after Bob's memorial service, I went to a writing retreat at The

Clearing Folk School in Door County, Wisconsin. The Clearing was a perfect place to go after everyone left and my home was filled with loneliness. I stayed in a cabin with five other women and all the students ate together family style in a beautiful rustic dining hall. As I roamed the 128 acres of Door County forests and meadows edged by cliffs towering over the Green Bay part of the Great Lake, I planned to write Volume II of *Visions from Two Continents*. Volume I was at the publishers. My instructor, Roger Kuhns said, "Make a story arc."

I scribbled one sad incident after another, constantly looking up out the window at the trees waving to me. I was getting nowhere; I made the arc for Volume I. It told the history of the USA and Australia from 1912 to 1955 through the eyes of my mother, Sheila Buchanan Buell. It had a definite story line, goal, conflict, and resolution. Only the resolution in 1955 never happened. Sheila did not take her family back to her home in Australia. Volume II would be a story of depression and disappointment; I couldn't write it.

Roger said, "Tell me about your life."

I said, "Oh I didn't have a very interesting life, I've gotten beyond all the problems and I'm happy now." Except, of course, I was very lonely, but I didn't say that.

"Tell me about it. How did you do that? Make a story map of your life," he said, giving me a direct assignment.

I sat down with a large sheet of paper and scribbled an outline of this book, amazed at all the ups and downs, the angels along the way that helped me learn and grow. I shuffled my way into a private meeting with Roger, wanting to hide behind my scribbled story arc. "This is pretty crazy. I don't know if anyone will believe this or want to read it," I said, my eyes averting his straight-on gaze.

He smoothed the large sheet of paper on the table and read it very carefully. "There is a lot here," he said, his voice reflecting the paper with kind empathy. "This is the story you need to tell."

The tension in my shoulders relaxed, "Thanks," I said. "I know I need to tell this story. I just wasn't sure when, or if it would be believed."

"Now is the time," he said with a conviction, that inspired me with a force to carry it beyond the room, to share it with the class, and write this book.

I started writing. In 2018 I took the planned honeymoon trip with a girlfriend to Australia, sharing *Visions from Two Continents Vol I* with my Australian family and the historical society in Peachester, Queensland. I returned there in 2019 and again in 2020.

Before I left for Australia in February of 2020, I must have had a premonition. I scanned all the documents pertaining to this story into my computer: the articles that I'd written for the Meditation Center, the research papers I'd gotten from the Greens at the Menninger Research Foundation, the journals from our two retreats in Minnesota, the letters from so many women, stories of abuse, and the thank you notes from people who had joined the healing network. I packed my computer and brought it along even though I only planned to stay in Australia three months.

When the global pandemic hit in March, I stayed in Australia for fifteen months. Most of the time I was writing, confined to a farm next door to where my mother had grown up, drawn there by the stories she told me about this place. I communicated with the outside world like a character in an Asimov sci-fi novel.

Thankful for the magic of the internet, I connected with Indriani, a fellow victim of Swami Rama, telling her about my project.

"Haven't you gotten beyond that?" Indriani asked in a message, concerned that I was dealing with trauma.

I wanted to jump back from that text. It had been such a long struggle getting beyond… *That's what the book is about. It is the journey of getting beyond all that.* I wrote back, feeling a need to defend myself.

The contacts and materials brought back all the memories, but I still couldn't remember the outcome of the case. What happened after the appeal? I asked Indriani, Peter, Debbie, Phil, and Dan but they didn't know either.

I searched online for information about Swami Rama. I found his volumes of books, many written by assistants such as Dan, hoping to become enlightened. Then I came across "The 100 Year Experiment in Eastern Spirituality" (prem-rawat-bio.org), This article put my friends and me among many other followers of different "gurus." Swami Rama was the 23rd guru in the list. Almost all of them used their teaching of eastern philosophy to fill their pockets and/or use women. This article painted the "guru" culture as a cult promotion, giving human beings more power than they could safely use.

My experiences with Swami Rama led me to the conclusion that humans like to put others on a pedestal where they can promote themselves, claiming they are pursuing a higher good, while using ordinary humans as slaves to their desires of wealth and pleasure. I always wanted to find a real enlightened human, but if there was one, I don't think they would want to tell anyone. If *I* was enlightened, I would not tell anyone.

When I was in a leadership position at the Meditation Center, I felt the power of being regarded as enlightened. I didn't like it at all. It felt wrong. I knew that, although I could put myself in a relaxed state and twist my body in strange positions, I wasn't any better than anyone else. I learned I'm on a path, I felt a higher presence, and it was personal. I believed each person had their own path. It was not my place to tell them how to pursue their higher power.

The guru article did help me find my answer; it linked to the results of the trial and appeal (link to http://prem-rawat-bio.org/nrms/info/94v1118.pdf). Even though it was 40 pages long, I sat down and read every word.

The case told the story of the young girl, Jasmine whose family believed Swami Rama was a totally pure and enlightened soul who would protect their daughter. She was trained, starting at age 14, to obey her guru Swami Rama, only to be raped and used for his sexual pleasure.

My heart reached out to her family when they tried, like so many before them, to get the Himalayan Institute to acknowledge what had been happening to women in their facility. But they, like so many before them, were banished and ignored. They were brave to bring this before the court.

Jasmine's family produced reams of testimony and won. Then Swami Rama died in India and the Himalayan Institute appealed. The suit left out the struggles that came before, our story that started in the 1970s. If the laws had been different in the 1970s it might all have ended, then. Many souls would not have spent years of their lives defending a lie.

In their appeal claim, the Himalayan Institute said the Institute was not liable. They didn't defend Swami Rama - that case was lost. They were only interested in their financial liability.

But the judge ruled not only that they were they liable, he also fined them additional damages!

I was so surprised that I had to read it numerous times. I just didn't expect that outcome. I forwarded this paper to Debbie and Phil, Indriani, Peter, Dan and Shanti. None of them had seen it. They too were happy to have the resolution, at last. After being ignored and shamed for years, even if we weren't the ones winning the suit, at least we'd won the argument.

Unfortunately, the story isn't just about one guru in an eastern tradition. It's about all of us who wanted to defend a charismatic personality because we'd been manipulated to believe they promoted a "greater good".

Finally, I've come to understand that laws can promote equality and transparency, instead of creating loopholes for those in power. In our democracy we have taken away the God-power of kings, but human beings still continue to want to put other humans on a pedestal and blindly follow them. It isn't good for the person put on high, because it empowers predatory behavior and disarms the vulnerable followers.

Post Script

Bob is still there in my heart. No matter where I go, he is with me. Our relationship was one of the lucky ones. We learned and we grew, willing to work on ourselves, which ultimately led to a relationship that lasted over 50 years counting the two years that we were engaged. I'm ever thankful for the years we spent together, through thick and thin, in sickness and in health, working, playing, growing, and multiplying, blessed with two wonderful children.

The Greek philosopher Heraclitus said, "The only thing that is constant in this world is change." My husband, although he abides in my heart, he is not at my side. My children have grown and left home for lives of their own. The community at the Camper Resort on Lake Travis has dispersed, life there disrupted by a flood. Thanks to one person's efforts we still have a Facebook page, a place to communicate. Communication and caring are keys to the joy in life. We need to keep the doors open wide and not let anyone or anything slam them shut.

"Make new friends but keep the old: Those are silver, these are gold," was a poem written over a century ago by Joseph Parry. But in my mind, it comes out as a song sung by Mr. Rogers. When I've been moving from place to place, I've tried to keep in touch with friends new and old. Sometimes a friend closes the door and doesn't want to communicate since I'm not there any more. It breaks my heart. I let go and take a deep breath, allowing the fresh air to fill every part of my being. A walk in the woods or the bush brings me to a meditative state closer to God, healing my soul.

My goals in this life have changed. I'm no longer an individual soul seeking God but a human seeking constructive relationships with other humans and the natural world. I use the yoga techniques I learned to stay flexible and to calm myself (when I remember to use them). To me, meditation is a walk in the woods, time sitting down in the Australian bush or the Wisconsin woods, actively being there helping to protect native plants by pulling out invasive weeds. Weeds just like the weeds of self-judgement, loneliness and isolation that crop up in my life.

I love attending a church service with wonderful music that helps me explore the world within in communion with others.

In this book I've shared my experience, strength, and hope, despite my initial embarrassment at doing so. My dream is, that others may benefit from my experience. I have used first names or changed the names of many people in the book and tried to contact everyone mentioned in this book. I make no judgements of other people except to say that some experiences are hurtful, and I hope we learn to respect each other and protect our children.

Life is a journey, hopefully where each of us will grow to achieve progress towards positive lasting relationships, with ourselves, each other, and the natural world. I've been continuing that journey through writing, family, travel, nurturing the environment, and developing new relationships. That's for another book, maybe a fiction book. Reality is sometimes too strange to be believed.

Bibliography

ACA Handbook Committee, *Adult Children of Alcoholic/Dysfunctional Families*, Torrance, CA. 2006

Boyd, Doug. *Swami Encounters with Modern Mystics* published by The Himalayan International Institute of Yoga Science and Philosophy of the USA. Honesdale, Pennsylvania

Darling, Patricia. "Turning East in the Twin Cities: Converts and Movements in the 1970s' PhD Thesis, the University of Minnesota

Igunait, Rajmani. *Swami Rama of the Himalayas: His Life and Mission* published by The Himalayan International Institute of Yoga Science and Philosophy of the USA. Honesdale, Pennsylvania

Jones, Roger. *Journal of the Ashram Retreat of Dyana-Mandiram*, St. Croix Park, Minnesota15-22 August 1971, unpublished.

Johnson, Vernon E. *I'll Quit Tomorrow*, HarperCollins, New York, 1973.

Tameling, Rainer. *Autogenic Training developed by Dr. J. H. Schutz and Progressive Relaxation developed by Edmund Jacobson:Two Paths to Relaxation* March 23, 2015

Vanaskie, Thomas I. Trial Verdict V:3CV-94-1118, Jasmine Patel vs. Himalayan International Institute of the USA. Memorandum of case Sept 4, 1997 accessed April 24, 2022 via http://prem-rawat-bio.org/nrms/info/94v1118.pdf

Webster, Katharine. *The Case Against Swami Rama* by Yoga Journal Nov/Dec 1990. Accessed April 24, 2022 via http://www.katharinewebster.com/Text/kw0003.pdf

Wilcox, Bradford W. *The Evolution of Divorce*, Fall, 2009, National Affairs, accessed April24, 2022, nationalafffairs.com.